TURNING OVER STONES

First Published in Great Britain 2016 by Mirador Publishing

First edition: 2016

A copy of this work is available through the British Library.

ISBN: 978-1-911044-46-8

Mirador Publishing
Mirador
Wearne Lane
Langport
Somerset
TA10 9HB

Turning Over Stones

By

Michael Haley

Introduction

What's it all about?

    I said in the introduction to my previous little poetry book, "An Idea Appeared" that I'd been writing poems and songs since I was a spotty teenager, and stories perhaps since I was a wrinkly pensioner. Therefore I decided to attempt to compile and edit all of my writings of any quality from the very beginning up to the present day.

    In the interim I had previously put together a little collection of poems and songs illustrating the full range of my creations, and that was what became "An Idea Appeared".

    I hope that you enjoyed that little collection as an aperitif, or an hors d'oeuvres, or even an amuse bouche?

    If you did, then maybe that is why you are reading this now.

    Many thanks for coming back.

    I have been assembling this complete collection over a long period of time, and the project seemed to grow exponentially. So eventually I decided to convert it into 3 separate undertakings.

    Volume 1 is this collection titled "Turning Over Stones" 1949 to 1998.

    The title comes from a song which I wrote the lyric for in July,1998. But it also serves to illustrate the process I have been going through to uncover (hopefully) all my gems.

    Volume 2 will be "Tall Words on a Wall" 1998 to 2004.

    This title derives from the final song lyric of this compilation which was written on 6th June, 2004 to be published later on this year.

    Volume 3 will be "Walls Come Tumbling Down" 2004 to the present day.

    The title just seems at this moment in time to be an appropriate one for what happened in the world and in my life since 2004. This will be published in 2017.

    Maybe this collection is a biography or maybe it's a chronology.

    Maybe it's a bit of both?

There is a lot more to come in the other 2 volumes covering poems, songs, stories and recording history up to the present time.

Pulling it all together

As far as I can remember I started assembling the 3 volumes in September 2014, pulling together items from here, there and everywhere. Sometimes I had no computer records, and had to retype stuff in from my hand-written scribblings. I trawled through the past darkly finding little gems, discarding fool's gold, and being tough on myself for what should and should not be included. It has been an interesting and emotional roller coaster ride through my literature history.

Obviously, I didn't start writing on the day that I was born. It appears that the first time I kept something I had written was in 1965 when I wrote the song, "I Remember the Summer and You".

The reason that this finds itself in chapter 5, "Aspire if you Dare", is because the preceding 4 chapters, the contents of which were constructed many years later, cover a period from 1949 to 1965. Therein lies the contention, or is it confusion, that this maybe either a biography or a chronology. However, throughout the construction I have attempted to place everything in as logical an order as possible.

Looking back I would say that the long ago immediate trigger for becoming a writer over a period of over 50 years seems to be have been the acquisition of a guitar, and the subsequent learning to play the instrument creating a desire to pen my own songs. This is borne out by the fact that my standard method of song writing has always been to write a poem and then set it to music.

During the intervening period the creation of "products of the pen" has waxed and waned many times leading to many barren Sahara eras interspersed with prolific Amazon rain forest epochs.

After spending over 30 years writing practically all poems and songs (none of which had ever been recorded up to that point) I did finally undertake something more substantial in 1998.

How did this come about?

In May 1996 I had my first heart attack, and after tests was advised that I would need a bypass operation. This was eventually scheduled for December

1997, but before that time arrived I had another heart attack in November 1997 while playing golf in France. After my recovery from the bypass surgery I wrote a book called "Taking Chances, Making Choices", detailing my experiences. The writing and editing processes took about 2 years, but sadly this work was never published. No thanks are due to the British Heart Foundation. The book was part biography, part diary, and part good advice for fellow heart patients.

However in "Turning Over Stones" I use extracts from the book "Taking Chances, Making Choices", having removed the cardiac advice elements to create a more coherent and focussed biography. In reality the biography fizzles out in 1997/8, and what you are left with then from that point on is a range of different pieces mostly poems and songs. Later on I started to write stories and novels.

All of the writings illustrate what was on my mind at the times, and colour in moods, ups and downs, topical and personal events, and also chart my recording history.

What I have tried to do throughout the compilation is to put each individual item in context with a short introductory sentence or paragraph so that you can sense where I'm coming from.

Enjoy!

Index - Turning Over Stones

CHAPTER 1

You've Never had it so Good

"Extensive research reveals that,
walls do not have ears,
but they do have sausages."

Since this is a compilation of writings in biographical order I think the best way for me to begin is with some information about my childhood years covering the period from 1949 to 1959. In the late 1990's I wrote an unpublished book titled "Taking Chances, Making Choices". The inspiration for this endeavour came from my need to record my experiences after a heart attack in 1996, and it took me about 2 and a half years to write it. Unfortunately the British Heart Foundation were uninterested in helping me to get the book published. Here are a few extracts from the book.

Taking Chances, Making Choices

CHAPTER 1

In the Beginning
A short brisk walk through my life from 1949 to 1959

1949 was an eventful year. The Berlin Airlift ended when Stalin backed down and withdrew the blockade after 11 months. Russia tested an atomic bomb, and In China, the civil war resulted in victory for Mao Sae Tung's Communists. British troops were sent to Hong Kong as a show of strength. The Cold War began, and the world feared Communist domination.

At home, sweets and clothes were taken off ration. The Labour government nationalised major industries including Coal, Gas, Railways, and Electricity, and the Welfare State was established with the National Health Service as its cornerstone.

At No. 47, Melville Road, Rainham, Essex, I was one of 750,000 babies born every year in the UK. Brought into the world by Dr. Stevens, with the umbilical cord wrapped tightly around my neck, I arrived in the "best room"; the front parlour of my grandmother's terraced cottage...

My mother, Gerda Erica Martha was born in 1920, and was a "war bride", who arrived in England from Germany in 1947. She came from the small but historically significant town of Spandau, on the outskirts of Berlin, at the confluence of the rivers Spree and Havel; tributaries of the Elbe. After WW2 when partition was completed Spandau was to find itself in the British Sector of

West Berlin, but only a few miles from the border with the German Democratic Republic (East Germany). The town has only one dubious claim to fame, in that it became synonymous with the prison there, which housed the Nazi war criminal Rudolph Hess until his death in the 1980's...

My father, Maurice John, (Jack) was born in 1927 in Saffron Walden, the eldest son of a family of 8 children. Soon after his birth the family moved to what was then the small village of Rainham in Essex, where the claims for recognition begin (and almost end!) with a Norman church; the church of St. Helen and St. Giles, built in the 12th century, and founded by Richard de Lucy, the son-in-law of Henry II.

My parents met when my father was serving as a British soldier in the Royal West Kent Regiment, and he was stationed in Berlin as part of the occupation forces after the Second World War. In 1947 they were married in the historic Rainham church...

Thanks for the memories

My sister Marion was born in January 1951, and then after moving from Melville Road, we shared a house with a large Indian family in Pennerly Road Rainham, only a mile or so from the River Thames. The proximity to the river gave me my earliest memory. Foggy or "smoggy" winter days were common in the early 50's before the Clean Air Act, and shortly after the move to this house, I can remember lying in my cot, and hearing the foghorns of ships on the river, plying their way into or out of the London Docks, which would have been in their heyday. In my early baby language, I called the Indians "Lo-Los"; perhaps because that was my interpretation of all they ever said to me. In their Indian accent "Hello!" or perhaps "Allo!" sounded to me like "Lo-lo!"

In 1952 my sister Sylvia was born in this house.

In 1953, when Elisabeth II became Queen, we moved to a new council house, at 36, Ennerdale Avenue, in a then slightly rural "village", of Elm Park, about 3 miles from Rainham and quite close to the famous wartime airfield at Hornchurch Aerodrome...

What's in a name?

As a child I had a number of distinct disadvantages, which served to provide the early foundation to my character and personality. I was born with a congenital ptosis of the right eye inherited from my father, which in those days was called a "lazy eye". When I was 2 years old, my father and me went to a hospital in East Grinstead, where the eminent pioneer plastic surgeon, Sir Archibald McIndoe, attempted to correct both our lazy eyes. This surgeon had risen to fame, by ground breaking new techniques to treat the horrific wounds of unfortunate victims of the 2nd World War, but my little problem proved too much for his prominent and undoubted expertise.

Despite a sizeable influx of German born war brides in the late Forties and early Fifties the post war hatred of Nazism, and the natural British propensity for xenophobia was rampant. In addition British people had not yet learned to separate German from Nazi.

My common facial imperfection and my part German ancestry when combined with a weak, pale, and skinny frame, was more than enough ammunition for the simplistic outlook and cruel cynicism that only children seem to be able to master in finding a basis for ridicule.

So I became "Skinny Nazi one-eye".

In one unfortunate incident at Dunningford's Junior School, somebody had scribbled "All Nazis must die", on the wall outside the school entrance. Mr James, the headmaster, who was a dour, dark-featured authoritarian character, exhibited a typical misunderstanding, and over-reacted to this trivial event when he summoned all the children of mixed German/British descent to his office, and severely reprimanded this confused and totally innocent group...

Shepherds and sweets

At Christmas the school presented the traditional nativity play, and I had a non-speaking part as one of the 3 shepherds. Mum made me an orange crepe paper shepherd's suit, and the teacher provided a decorated bamboo stick as a shepherd's rook. Many of the parents in the early evening audience may have wondered why one of the shepherds found it difficult to keep still when on stage. Their doubts were probably quelled when a puddle appeared where I was standing and my crepe paper clothes begun to disintegrate. The cast were all in stockinged feet or open sandals, and many of them trod in the puddle as they left the stage. In between scenes the caretaker mopped up the unexpected downpour, and neither Jesus, Mary, Joseph nor any of the wise men realised they had been upstaged by a more up to date drama occurring behind them...

With paper?

It was difficult for many of the children in class to bear the embarrassment of asking to go to the toilet during a lesson. And can you imagine the trepidation, if it was necessary, to use their euphemism, to visit to the toilet "with paper". That was the cue for the teacher to dole out two sheets of Izal, just to ensure that everyone knew where you were going. I lost count of the number of times I nearly disgraced myself in school, and on several occasions the worst did happen. Even going to the toilet "with paper" between lessons required the formal request to the teacher to provide the standard issue of 2 non-absorbent, rough and ill-designed for its purpose, sheets of Izal...

Glimpses of childhood

Sundays was always a special day. Mum would make sure we had a proper roast dinner, followed by fruit for afters. The memory of what roast beef used to smell like when it was permeating the house with its glorious aroma, stays with me today. As does the delicious taste of beef dripping on toast for tea, although the experience is impossible to imitate today with what is laughingly now called dripping, tasting like paraffin and candle wax.

In the afternoon Mum baked cakes and that filled our home with another wonderful and equally memorable fragrance. My sisters and I, in time honoured fashion would fight about who was going to lick the bowl that the cake mixture was made in.

Around teatime Robin Hood was the favourite programme on our Ferguson telly, a 9-inch black and white screen, but the size of a modern tumble dryer. Remembering all the classic Fifties children's programmes is easy, even though nowadays they would all probably make the Tellytubbies look sophisticated.

What was the relationship between the little weed and those Flowerpot men?

What did Andy Pandy do in that box with Loopy Lou?

Can there have ever been so inept a puppeteer, as the unique incompetent who pulled the strings on Muffin the Mule?

British TV had a lot to learn from the Americans, who provided some saving graces in the quality of children's programmes with such gems as Roy Rogers and Trigger, and, the Lone Ranger and Tonto...

We all had a bath, once a week every Sunday, whether we needed it or not!

There was no central heating in the house, just a coal fire in the grate, which had a back boiler providing the hot water in winter. In summer, when the fire was not in use, there was a copper gas boiler to heat up the water, which we would carry up to the bathroom in buckets and bowls. For the sake of economy and convenience the 3 of us kids, my 2 younger sisters and me, would share the bath water. Mum said as I was the oldest, I would be bathed last of the 3, but I had the privilege of kicking the water out towards the plughole. At bedtime on Sundays, there was always the beautiful cool sensation of getting into bed, (made with sheets and blankets) after the bath.

Broken family

Mum and Dad were always arguing, and Mum always won every battle, while Dad seemed to be constantly irritable and bad-tempered shouting at us from his bedroom window after yet another week of night work. Suddenly, my dad had his own food cupboard and fixed his own meals; as he was sent to Coventry in his own home. My most vivid childhood image of my dad was a man in brown corduroy trousers, and a cloth cap arriving home from work at the Murex factory in Rainham on his bike. Many years later in my 20's, whenever I found myself in the polluted atmosphere around the Rainham/Purfleet area, I could catch the whiff of the Van de Berg and Jurgen's margarine factory. This was a sort of sickly, oily chemical odour which even today still reminds me of my dad.

When I was 7 my parents decided to call it a day after years of friction and argument. Dad didn't say much, and 3 innocent kids stood at the door waving him goodbye totally unaware of the seriousness of the situation. It was only when we learned that he had taken the precious Ferguson TV that we all cried...

War and remembrance

My earliest memories of world events covered by news broadcasts on our new Regentone telly, relate to events that bore certain similarities. In 1956 I remember seeing the Russian tanks crushing rebellion in Hungary, and British troops on alert in Egypt after General Nasser seized control of the Suez Canal.

Britannia, despite being smashed by 6 years of war, still ruled the waves. Gunboat diplomacy still frightened the peasants witless throughout the uncivilised world. To be British was to be proud to ponder over all the pink bits on maps of the world, and to know that you were privileged to be born and raised in the small island that so expertly came to dominate (exploit), and develop (plunder) the largest empire humanity had ever seen.

Safe and Clean

In the 50's streets were safe places to play. There were so few cars, and we played football, cricket, and rounders in the street with only minimal traffic interruption. Also, it was safe for children to go off on their own, and it was not unusual for me to spend all day in the park, wandering home just before it got dark. The small stream called the Ingrebourne ran through Harold Lodge Park from the Hornchurch end by the swimming pool to the Rainham end next to a large area of open land called the Chase. Every kid was told "Don't go and play in the Chase, there are bad men there!". But the river ran through there as well as the park, and it was wild and uncultivated, often populated by grazing horses. We went there anyway. It was infinitely more exciting!

At least once a week in the endless eternally warm and sunny childhood summers, I would trudge home the one mile from either the park or the Chase, boots squelching water, after falling in the river again, while swinging on a rope, or trying to jump from bank to bank. At least I was getting 2 baths a week!

Bonfires

In late October every year we busied ourselves for a few days, making an effigy of Guy Fawkes out of old clothes and newspapers and a papier-mâché mask, and then carried this dummy down to Elm Park station because it was "Penny for the Guy" time. People were much poorer, but also more generous, and the sight of a few scruffy kids, indulging in some legitimate begging outside the station usually meant that more than the odd penny was tossed. On a good night, we could go home with 2 shillings...

Presents, puppies and puffs of smoke

I never got a guitar as a Christmas present, but I did have a Hornby clockwork train set, and some plasticine. At Christmas we always had an enormous real tree taking up half the room, dressed in German style, with metal clipped candleholders, and proper wax candles. Filling our house with the pungent smell of pine needles, mixed with the candle wax burning, and culminating on Christmas morning, when the extra exciting flavours of oranges or tangerines and chocolate were added.

Mum followed the German St. Nicholas tradition, where on 6th December Santa Claus made a quick reconnaissance visit, and if you left your shoes highly polished outside your bedroom door, he would fill them with nuts and oranges, and a sixpenny piece, provided you had been good...

Whenever mum took us the Elm Park shopping centre, we waited with anticipation for the characteristic low rumbling sensation in the ground, which we knew to be the unmistakable sound of a steam train approaching the station. We would run to the top of the bridge to see the train, and to stand and breathe in that wonderful coal and sulphur, bad-eggy smell of the smoke as the train chugged and sweated its way to its next stop at Upminster or Barking.

Trolley buses

I was the first grandchild to be presented to my grandmother, and she doted on me. Her "hobby" was shopping, and quite often she would take me with her, on her expeditions. I hated the shopping, but the travelling about to new and exciting places was very educational. "Nanna" came from Gravesend in Kent, just a short boat trip across the River Thames from Tilbury, and I had many an adventure crossing the river as I accompanied her on shopping pilgrimages there. Her favourite shopping centre seemed to be in Barking, (still in Essex in those days), and this provided the wonderful experience of travelling on the smooth, almost silent, and ecologically friendly, trolley buses that comprised the main transport method in that area. After their abandonment as a preferred vehicle, I was sad at the passing of this brilliant mode of transport.

Ooh Matron!

When I was 6, we made lots of visits to Moorfield's Eye Hospital in London, and I remember the fascination of travelling on underground trains, and the peculiar, nose-itching smell of ozone produced by the electric trains on the London Underground. After a series of examinations both myself and my sister Marion were admitted to Moorfield's for similar eye operations. Mine was the second attempt at putting my droopy eyelid right. Although Marion was there at the same time as me, it was a distressing and brutal experience. Matron ruled OK, and nobody argued...

I do like to beside the seaside

We had our first ever holiday in 1957, at Leysdown on the Isle of Sheppey, in Kent, journeying there in an open topped car owned by a work colleague of my mum. The Dartford crossing wasn't even a glimmer in some enterprising planner's eyes then, and neither was the M2, and for some reason our driver preferred to take the Woolwich Ferry, rather than the Tilbury to Gravesend crossing. So the journey to our crude holiday chalet, with no electricity, and therefore serviced entirely by Calorgas, for cooking, heating and light, took nearly all day. Whenever we were indoors, and especially at night, there was that strangely comforting hot metal and burning paint smell of Calorgas. Staying by the seaside for a whole week, playing on what was then an unpolluted beach where you could still collect shells, more than compensated for the "cruel penance" of having to live on potatoes fried in lard, eggs, and banana sandwiches...

The early Fifties was a time of austerity and post war uncertainty, but we did have free school milk and school dinners. Then in 1959, Harold Macmillan told us "You've never had it so good", and I'm sure we all echoed back, "What do you mean, Harold, we've never had it at all!"

CHAPTER 2

Remember Road and the Ragamuffin Boy

"He wore a snotty nose with pride,
His hand me down, jumble sale clothes could not be denied,
His shoes were 2 sizes too big, his laces untied,
He was standing bedraggled in the freezing rain,
And never, ever easily cried."

Talking Remember Road Blues

Well over 10 years after finishing "Taking Chances, Making Choices" I wrote the song, Talking Remember Road Blues while I was on a Creative Writing Course at the Friary in Maldon. The work, originally entitled the Walnut Project, was required to have a Christmas theme. I only just managed to satisfy that criterion, but when the song was performed at the writing group in December 2011, it was enthusiastically received. Clearly, the song covered much of the same territory of childhood memories as I outlined in the unpublished book" Taking Chances, Making Choices".

I employed the concepts of a talking blues where the song is constructed with verses and choruses as standard, but after every verse or two there is additional dialogue which is presented as if it was an ad lib comment.

Written 22nd November, 2011

Let me take you for a stroll down Remember Road
and a walk across Nostalgia Square;
For a winding wander down Memory Lane -
to pick my forget-me-nots there.

Do you remember when Christmas didn't start in September,
just after the summer return?
When Bonfire night was just one night,
for everybody's big bang and big burn?
We'd hardly heard of Halloween;
there was no Trick or Treat,
And nobody needed to be frightened at night
when walking down the street.

Back in the days when Christmas came in December
we had a real tree with candles to light.
There were strange smells like tangerines and chocolate
arriving on Christmas Eve night.
Believe it or not, Christmas dinner was just chicken,
and everyone enjoyed the sprouts (twice!),
And when I loosened a tooth on the sixpence in the Christmas pudding
 the tooth fairy still came out.

When I was 6 I was in the school nativity play.
I was ! of the 3 shepherds
all dressed in orange crepe paper outfits.
Just before Jesus was born
the shepherds were standing in puddle -
after somebody pee'd them self on stage.
Yes! It was me!

Let me take you for a stroll down Remember Road
and a walk across Nostalgia Square;
For a winding wander down Memory Lane -
to pick my forget-me-nots there.

Do you recall, when we all had to walk to school,
and the cardboard in our shoes was getting wet;
When there was free school milk in the morning,
and school dinners were the best meal you'd get;
When we learned our 12-times table from a blackboard,
and went home covered in chalk dust;
Were you around when we had pounds, shillings and pence,
and it made good sense to us?

When you slept in a bed made with sheets and blankets
and in the winter your Dad's overcoat as well?
We only had warmth in the living room.
Do you remember that cosy glow and coal fire smell?
We still went to school in the winter snows,
never mind the weather, and no matter what;
You shared the bath water with the whole family -
once a week whether you needed it or not.

Because I had 4 sisters I always went into the bath last.
Sometimes, I came out more dirty than when I went in.
And I got the blame for the dirty ring around the bath afterwards.

Let me take you for a stroll down Remember Road
and a walk across Nostalgia Square;
For a winding wander down Memory Lane -
to pick my forget-me-nots there.

We might go scrumping for apples, play Knock down Ginger,
or a million other pranks and tricks,
Go to Saturday Morning Pictures,
or to Woolworths to nick the pick-n-mix.
The barbershop was in the back of Finlay's tobacconist;
short back-and-sides the only choice,
Because Sir might want "something for the weekend",
women weren't allowed in with the boys.

What a treat to go Southend on a steam train;
excitement rising as the sea drew near;
We had bags of chips, candyfloss, watched Punch and Judy,
and walked to the end of the pier.
For hours long we played in the sewage outfall,
and ate sandwiches made by Mum's fair hand,
And went home contented with seaweed between our toes,
and pockets full of shells and sand.

Once a year we went to the Southend at night time,
when they switched the illuminations on.
In those days there was a place up on the cliffs
called Never Never Land,
festooned with fairy lights and cartoon characters,
and full of little waterfalls.
I wanted to live there,
and often refused to go home.

Let me take you for a stroll down Remember Road,
And a walk across Nostalgia Square,
For a winding wander down Memory Lane,
To pick my forget-me-nots there.

There was so little traffic around in the street;
you could safely play football, cricket, or tennis.
Indoors, we played Ludo, Snakes and Ladders, Tiddlywinks;
we were Beryl the Peril, or Dennis the Menace.
We all had good manners; said please and thank you,
excuse me and I'm sorry, and all with a smile,
And Father Christmas didn't have to be CRB checked
to make sure he wasn't a paedophile.

On Sundays we listened to the radio.
There was Family Favourites, and the Billy Cotton Band Show.
On the monochrome 9 inch telly we watched Robin Hood,
and Roger Moore was Ivanhoe.
The whole house was filled with that lovely smell
as Mum baked cakes,
And all us kids argued about who was going to lick the bowl.

So its certain my friends that life was surely much simpler then,
even if our table was bare.
There were no CDs, or DVDs, or LCD TVs,
no iPods, or mobile phones back there.
We communicated by stopping and talking face to face;
everyone had time to listen.
There was a gazunder under the bed;
we were lucky 'cause we did have a pot to piss in.

No Facebook, No Twitter, No Email,
No Internet, No Xbox, No eBay,
No Google, and certainly no pot noodle,
No political correctness, Thank God!
No money, scruffy clothes, no cars, a snotty nose,
no sweets, not much too eat.
But lots of love, and lots of fun,
and smiles from everyone.

Well we went for a stroll down Remember Road
and a walk across Nostalgia Square,
For a winding wander down Memory Lane -
to pick my forget-me-nots there.

Ragamuffin Boy (The Magic, the Madness and the Mystery)

About 15 years after writing "Taking Chances, Making Choices" I wrote this short story, which is a piece of blatant nostalgia with some poetical bits in it. But the Ragamuffin Boy obviously overlaps with many of the components and sentiments of pieces I had previously written elsewhere.

Written 28th September, 2012

Despite the name there were no trees in Ennerdale Avenue, but there were neat front gardens, and privet hedges. Number 36 had its own front door, painted red, and a back garden and outside toilet. The war was long over. At least to a child four years is a long time. And the world crept slowly out of its devastation like a snail slides determined across the pavement. The country was on its knees, unable to make ends meet without the most desperate of measures, but the people had already proved their indomitability, and they were not about to be undermined by rationing, shortages and deprivation. Nobody could have dared to declare that it was the best of times, but clearly it couldn't be the worst of times either.

And in the midst of his safe haven,
In a world of desolation,
Lived a ruffian, a ragamuffin boy;
A waif of a child, skinny, pale, undernourished, naive.
He wore a snotty nose with pride,
His hand me down, jumble sale clothes could not be denied,
His shoes were 2 sizes too big, his laces untied;
He was standing bedraggled in the freezing rain, and never, ever easily cried.
In a house where the cupboard was guarded by old mother Hubbard,
Yes! Always bare,
Austerity the daily norm; poverty the regime everywhere;
No shelter from the storm, careworn and forlorn,
He wandered puzzled down his homebound lanes, beneath the heavy skies.

Sometimes the longest summer arrived, and the summer rains were warm, and if there were thunder storms, he would hide under the table just as if it were an air raid. He learned to protect himself from the lightning by not holding metal things like knives, and by counting the time between lightning and thunder to know how far away the storm was. To survive.

He walked to school, come rain or shine, and walking in the fog was fun.

And when the winter snows fell he played outside with everyone, wearing a hand-knitted bobble hat, and fingerless gloves.

His shoes let the water in until his toes were frozen like icicles, and that's when the snowman building and snowball fighting had to stop. Then, he'd go indoors to a coal fire; smelly, smoky, dirty, but always welcoming, and warm his toes on the hearth until they were fully thawed. Sundays were the favourite days, a weekly bath after the Sunday roast, and a hot water bottle for a nice warm bed.

In the early years at the Dunningford School,
He quickly learned the teacher's rules,
Got the slipper and the cane,
Broke the rules, felt the pain.

He hated school dinners, especially the everyday mashed potato and stewed cabbage, learned all his times tables, and discovered that all the girls were pretty except for Eileen Brown. But then he and she were the two smelliest, dirtiest, scruffiest kids in the school, and so the teacher always put them together for the last lesson on Fridays, which was country dancing. Worse still, at playtime Eileen always wanted to play kiss chase.

The child learned words and rhymes and useful phrases like:
Liar, liar, your pants are on fire, and,
Sticks and stones may break my bones, but names will never hurt me.
And then there was;
"Three dirty birds, sitting on the kerbs,
Chirpin' and a burpin' and eatin' dirty worms."
Or:

"Spring has sprung, the grass has riz,
I wonder where the birdies is,
Some people say the bird is on the wing, but that's absurd,
The wing is on the bird."

Times were hard, and the latch key kid went home to an empty house, and pulled the key on a string through the letterbox to let himself in. He made himself tea and toast, because his Mum was working at the factory, and his Dad had disappeared. Often at 5:30 he strolled the 100 yards to the bus stop in Rosewood Avenue, an avenue with trees, to meet his Mum off the 165 bus. The ragamuffin boy greeted her with a white mouse in his pocket, and an alarm clock to tell the time in his hand. The first question was always the same.

"What's for tea?"

Whatever it was, it was basic, inventive and filling, and given with the good advice of "Eat it all up, because that's all there is!"

At least Friday's were different. It was payday, and there was fish and chips, and if he was lucky the luxury of a banana or a small bar of chocolate. His dreams were punctuated with foody thoughts of R. Whites lemonade, Smith's crisps (with the little blue bag of salt), Jubblies and Old English Spangles.

And so, his apprenticeship was served with grazing knees, falling out of trees whilst scrumping or collecting conkers, and often spending all day in the park with Jimmy Saywood and Michael Broad just annoying the girls, but more often than not playing football or cricket.

He wasn't always alone in the house, but with a permanent absentee dad he was the only boy among 5 girls, including mum, big sisters, who were 8 and 10 years older, and little sisters who were 2 and 3 years younger.

In the ragamuffin boy's world people had names and jobs to do. There was the coalman, the milkman, the bread van, the rag and bone man, and the mobile shop that sold everything and came at 6 o'clock every evening. He knew it had arrived when the man hollered "Dickeeeeee Birrrrrrrrd's".

They were all happy, good people.

Then, there was the rent man, a grumpy, bad man, and when he came you had to go and hide, and pretend there was nobody home.

It was a time of simple pleasures, games played with paper, sticks, and stones, or flying a kite made from bamboo canes, brown paper, sticky tape and string. Then there were other more dodgy pursuits like scrumping, pulling up potatoes or rhubarb from the nearby farmer's fields, knock down ginger, penny for the guy, and bob a job week (even though he wasn't in the scouts). And there were simple games like snakes and ladders, ludo, jacks, fivestones, hopscotch, and watching the girls play with skipping ropes.

He loved going to his Nanna's house all by himself on the bus, and especially eating a bag of chips on the top deck of the bus on the way home, feeling very grown up and a bit scared at the same time. To have a ride in a car was exciting, and to ride in Uncle Ronnie's timber lorry was even better.

The big sisters liked the new music played on their gramophone. Rock and roll WAS the new Rock and roll. Elvis was stuck somewhere called Heartbreak Hotel and then went to jail but still happily sang about it. Somebody pleaded not to step on his blue suede shoes, somebody else found his thrill on Blueberry Hill, and yet another fella confused him by singing be bopa Lula she's my baby.

Yes, the ragamuffin boy's days were filled with fun and adventure, the years were like millennia, and there was always a magic in the air. Not least of all when a brief glimpse of plenty was fuelled by the magic of believing in Father Christmas.

Dotted amongst the magic there was a world of madness where all at once everything seemed to be inside out, upside down, and back to front, and everybody just muddled along from day to day.

Through it all, hope was sustained by the mystery of all the wonderful experiences that lay ahead in the life of a ragamuffin boy.

That boy was me, and still is. No longer smelly and dirty, I hope! And also not so naive! Many, many years later, in a very different world, and armed with all the priceless wealth of experience, the magic still endures, the madness still perplexes, and the mystery still continues to fascinate.

CHAPTER 3
The Boy Becomes a Man
"They threw a wall around us all,
To keep us on their side,
And we weren't allowed to wave to the folks,
Who lived on the other side."

Taking Chances, Making Choices

CHAPTER 3

The Boy becomes a Man - Quickening my stride through 1959 to 1969

Time to move on

To my mother's abject disappointment I failed my 11+ exam after being so worried that I wet the bed the night before; and so in 1960 I was "condemned" to attend an ordinary secondary school, rather than a posh grammar or technical "High" school. After much pleading and promising to behave myself, my mother acceded to my choice, as the Sutton's school in Hornchurch, rather than the much nearer Britton's school only half a mile away. Economic reasons also had to be considered, as attending Sutton's required travelling the one stop on the train from Elm Park to Hornchurch. That was until mum could afford to buy me a bike, and then I could ride to school. Clever little sod, wasn't I?…

School Scrapes

After we moved to Brentwood I attended the St Martin's Boys School in Hanging Hill Lane; almost like a tastefully developed country lane. Once again we were in a semi rural setting, but although we were housed on a huge council estate the surrounding areas towards Brentwood itself consisted mostly of much posher private homes, including the select enclave of Hutton Mount. Moving just before Easter 1961, the air was full of the scent of blossom on the trees from the surrounding tree-lined avenues. The air smelled fresh and clean, and not far from our front door the development petered quickly out into open countryside again. This was the height of the Cold War; Khrushchev posturing with shoe banging at the UN, and Kennedy retorting with "Ich bin ein Berliner!" Sadly JFK was not aware that that he had just proclaimed to the world that he was a biscuit?

Soon President Kennedy would issue orders for Cuba to be blockaded in the escalating missile crisis. But teenage boys have more important things in mind. At St Martin's the boy's school shared the school fields with the girl's school of the same name next door. Our teacher, Jones the geography, slippered the whole class one summer afternoon when they arrived back late for a lesson on mining in Canada after the lunch break. All his hormone racing pupils had hung around in order to catch quick glimpses of "Juicy" June Williams doing the long jump long before the invention of sports bras...

My Back Pages

The feeling that the world would soon become a more liberated and friendly place, took a succession of serious blows when the news broke that Kennedy had been assassinated in November 1963, and that he had been replaced by a warmonger red-neck called Lyndon B, Johnson, who started sending American troops to Vietnam in 1964...

Displays of affection

At Shenfield Technical High School, typically for the way this school dealt with (blundered into!) everything, the same teacher who took chemistry and biology, handled the delicate area of sex education. When I was 15, Mr. Foot quivered terrified over diagrams of male and female parts, while everyone, both boys and girls sniggered as his ineptness, and then squirmed as he fenced off every relevant, but previously contrived to embarrass question.

Education had taken place in primary sexual behaviour much earlier, practising snogging, and French kissing, and undoing bra-clips, in the cloakrooms with Christine Galley, the most popular girl in the school.

What she wouldn't do for a bite of your Mars bar?...

Gimme Shelter

Down in a bus shelter opposite Kadwill's newsagents in Rayleigh Road, Hutton I was in a clinch with an early crush; a girl called Janet Robinson. Everybody knew her as Janet Fishshop because she lived over the local chippie run by her mum and dad. Janet had lank, mid-length, dark blonde hair which always smelled of last week's special fish supper, but she had a sexy and endearing lisp, and because she preferred to wear no shoes, her rather large feet always appeared as if she had just finished paddling on the mud-flats at Southend. Never mind, she was a great snog!

My trendy, up-to-date weekend wear consisted of the obligatory black leather jacket, a white t-shirt, very tight Lee Cooper ice blue jeans, and winkle-picker Chelsea boots. It was hot, and there was a rapidly developing bulge in my too tight jeans as on this balmy evening we practised heavy snogging. She only moved her hand a little, not even brushing me anywhere important, perhaps on my knee, but suddenly something exciting happened. Later that evening when I was undressing for bed, I discovered that my foreskin was stuck to my underpants with Evostick!...

Wild Thing

In the mid-60's we had pirate radio stations broadcasting off the Essex and Kent coasts, and best of all was Radio Caroline, featuring the embryonic talent of Kenny Everett in the Kenny and Cash programme. The BBC Light Programme and Home Service had previously monopolised the daytime airwaves, with the only beacon showing the future direction carried by the night-time only Radio Luxembourg. Radio Lux 208 enjoyed the twin irritations of only playing the first minute or so of every song, and always seeming to fade out of transmission just when the good bits were about to be sung. Early transistor radios were arriving from Hong Kong, although miniaturisation had only bought them down to the size of a book, and there was a rapidly developing and hugely exciting music scene...

Flicks

In my teens Saturday morning pictures had been replaced by Saturday Afternoon flicks mostly at the old cinema, (it may have been the Gaumont), in Brentwood, which was knocked down to make way for a new Woolworth's store in the late 60's. The attraction was the frequent showing of horror films from the Hammer House of Horror stable, all starring Christopher Lee as Dracula and Peter Cushing as his all-knowing adversary. Also, Edgar Alan Poe's doomy, morbid, and obsessional books were turned into equally single theme films, starring the elegant toned voice of Vincent Price, in such classics as The Raven, The Pit and Pendulum, and the convincingly scary (for it's time) Fall of the House of Usher...

Triumph, Tribulation, Trauma

At Shenfield Technical High School all pupils were subjected to unprecedented levels of intolerance, restriction and ritualised misunderstanding in order to further the single-minded ambitions of the senior teaching staff to achieve good GCE results with their first intake of pupils. They did, despite themselves, and to the immense credit of all the pupils!

At a time when attitudes throughout society were softening and the pop music revolution saw the Beatles and the Rolling Stones leading the way into a more liberated age this school insisted on silly uniforms including Eton-peaked caps even for 6th formers. Length of hair was always a contentious issue, and after my Mother found it necessary to write to Mr. Harry, about my hair having no bearing on my ability to learn, Hopeless Harry got his own back. After the school's first and very successful set of GCE results in 1965, the local rag; the Brentwood Gazette, came to take a picture of the senior staff and relevant pupils. I was still resplendent in my fringed Beatle haircut, and Mr. Harry refused to stand next to me in the photograph, and consigned me to the back row as far away from him as possible to ease his embarrassment. I had been one of only 3 pupils who had achieved 8 GCE passes at the first attempt with grades C and above.

A new level

Throughout my time at Shenfield Tech, up to the 5th form there was only a total class of 13, consisting of 9 boys and 4 girls. In the 6th form there were a total of 8 pupils, and I was the only 6th form pupil in Mildmay House. When the school sports day came around I was therefore obliged to compete in every event possible.

In the summer of 1965 after I'd achieved 8 "O" level GCE passes, I then succeeded in gaining another 2 in winter 1965...

On 20th August I began work as an Export Sales Correspondent for a company in Christopher Street EC2 called Gallenkamp, and after initial training became the "H" Section Correspondent, dealing with quotations, orders, distribution and shipping of all products in the company's extensive catalogue to several countries in the Middle East. One of my best customers was a company called Iraq Scientific, based in Baghdad; and I suppose I may have supplied them with various items that they employed in the Iraqi national nuclear weapons technology programme?...

Slow food

Although we had Wimpy Bars, a derivative of the 50's coffee shop with burgers, and some Little Chef outlets, the junk food revolution was in its infancy. Britain hadn't adopted the "fast food" tag yet. There were no international fast food dynasties like McDonald's, Burger King, Pizza Hut, and Kentucky Fried Chicken. Equally the pre-prepared ready meals which are now so popular were not yet available since the microwave had not become a fixture in every kitchen. In these pre snack pot days, two amazing convenient food products called the Vesta Beef Curry, and the Vesta Chow Mein were just arriving...

Down the Palais

For Essex kids the hotspot venue for dancing on Saturday Nights in 1966 was at the Ilford Palais, where they specialised in the latest Tamla Motown hits, the most memorable impact being made by the Four Tops, with hits like "Reach Out and I'll be There", and "Bernadette".

Beer glorious beer

After 17 years "in office", and after lengthy consideration among the Mandarins, 1966 saw Mao's cultural revolution taking place in China, and Watney's were quick to cash-in on this major event, with their own Red Revolution, by introducing the first keg beer, with their Red Barrel campaign.

Summer of Love

1967 will be long remembered as the best summer of the century up to that point, Later they labelled it "The Summer of Love", because flower power was wafting its way across the Atlantic, and there was a general feeling of better times around the corner for everyone. I was in love too, with my first real girlfriend, Denise, a petite and very attractive girl, with whom I had a relationship for over 6 months...

During the summer of love all was not peace and light. In May Israel fought and won the 6 day war against it's fractious Arab neighbours, and our government, in a rampant surge of paranoia, took the precaution of issuing petrol coupons just in case of oil shortages.

Every Bank Holiday the Mods and Rockers "fought" at Southend and other seaside resorts. But the reality was that most of the trouble was generated by restrictions on freedom of movement applied by an over-zealous police force.

Hair today, gone tomorrow

Problems with the length of my hair didn't disappear when I left school, even though in today's terms we are probably talking about a hair length no longer than that of Jonathan Ross or Julian Clary, it was still held by the next generation that hair should be army-short.

About a year after starting at Gallenkamp's, 11:00 am on a Friday morning arrived as usual with the much anticipated visit from the payroll office to hand out the pay packets; little brown envelopes with real notes and coins in them. Strangely, my pay packet was missing, and when I enquired as to its whereabouts I was advised that Keith Wilkinson, the department manager, wished to see me at 11:30.

Would I get a pay packet, so that I could go to The Flying Horse for the usual Friday lunchtime drink? Was I going to be sacked for some unknown reason?

"No!" I thought, "He's going to give me a pay rise!"

At 11:30 I knocked reverently on the manager's door, and then entered, striding across the path of green carpet that covered the huge distance from the door to his desk, and then stood by as he studied some papers before looking up at me, or should I say, through me, over metal framed glasses perched on the end of his pointy nose.

"Michael," he began, "Here's you pay packet, and when you've opened it you will find an extra half-a-crown in there."

"Yes! I've got a pay rise!" I thought.

He squashed that assumption quickly, "Michael, the extra half-a-crown is for your haircut" he sneered.

"But, I don't want a haircut," I replied quickly.

"Oh, I think you do! And I really would like you to take my opinion seriously," he replied

I understood that this wasn't a plea, it was an instruction.

After 2 pints of best bitter for Dutch courage in The Flying Horse, I reluctantly headed for the barbers, and had the most severe shearing possible, turning me into an early version of the skinhead. A creature held in such utter fear, loathing and disgust by the older generation; even more in disdain than the longhair.

Mr. Wilkinson, briefly left his office in the afternoon tea break, to inspect; took one look, and turned on his heel, slamming his office door shut as he scurried back to his safe refuge. Game set, and match to me!

I have a dream

Emancipation of the "blacks", not yet called Afro-Americans, in the US was blocked and stalemated by predictable dogma and in-bred racial hatred and misunderstandings. The civil rights movement gained momentum with Martin Luther King as its leading light, and many years later it's impossible not to recognise the power and charisma of this truly great man, especially in his much revered and often repeated "I have a dream" speech.

He knew he wouldn't be there to see it through!

Friends, flicks and going places

I had met Barry Childs; somebody who was to become a long time friend, during my love affair with Denise, and we had taken up trying to play the guitar together in late 1967. In early 1968 we took many an opportunity to use our rail season tickets to go to London at the weekends, and eventually found ourselves regularly visiting the Rose Morris music shop in Shaftesbury Avenue. Hours were often spent in there, just picking up expensive guitars and playing our 3 chords, with crude strumming or dodgy finger picking styles. One day I picked up a 12 string guitar and became mesmerised by its haunting, full bodied resonant sound; so different to the hollow empty tone of a 6 string acoustic. I had to have it!

During the next week a loan was negotiated with my sister Sylvia for the huge sum of 33 Guineas needed to acquire this EKO 12-string guitar; another life long friend.

Monty Pythons

The choice of David Frost to host the moon shot TV coverage was no accident, he was the most prominent and influential TV presenter of his day, spearheading the revolution in satirical comedy which complemented the

42

literary impact of Private Eye. Such programmes as "That Was the Week That Was", (TW3), perhaps owing its title to Harold Wilson's assertion that, "A week is a long time in politics", was followed up by "Not so much a programme, more a way of life", (NSMAPMAWOL) providing the jumping off platforms for many...

Giant leaps

Some weeks on the dole passed, being supplied by the State with the princely sum of £3 and 15 shillings a week (£ 3.75), before I rejoined an old work colleague from Gallenkamp, Brian Chamberlain, on 21st July 1969, working for a company called Phillips Petroleum U.K. Ltd. in Victoria.

It is easy to remember the day I started there because the previous night I had been glued to our monochrome television watching the Apollo 11 mission culminating in Neil Armstrong making his giant leap for mankind.

Colour telly was on the verge of introduction as a must rather than luxury, but most programmes were still only broadcast in monochrome, including the Moon Landing.

This momentous historical occasion, perhaps the most significant event of the 20th century was not echoed in my own life.

CHAPTER 4
Some of my Halcyon Days

"Keep that banner floating Frederic,
Keep that ensign high,
Hold that banner proudly Frederic,
Flying in the sky."

Swinging Sixties Talking Blues

The song "Swinging Sixties Talking Blues" was written while I was on a Creative Writing Course at the Friary in Maldon. The work was originally entitled the Doors Project, and I don't remember why. I was one of only two songwriters in the class and the remainder of those present were mostly writers of short stories. Realising that I was there for a different reason to the rest of the class, I thought I'd stick to the successful formula I'd used previously for the "Talking Remember Road Blues". Therefore I came up with a follow-up called "Swinging Sixties Talking Blues". Once again the song comes from my childhood and adolescent memories as I outlined in the unpublished book "Taking Chances, Making Choices". The talking blues is again constructed with verses and choruses as standard, but after every verse or two there is additional dialogue which is presented as if ad lib.

Written 21st December, 2011 to 4th January, 2012

Welcome to the swinging sixties; some of my halcyon days,
Though it was oh so long ago it still seems like yesterday.

In 1961 the Russians sent a man into space;
Yuri Gagarin he was called,
In April just for fun, strapped into Vostok1,
he spun around the world.
Then the Berlin Wall appeared overnight,
with guns and dogs installed,
And the free world stood there helpless
and watched the Iron Curtain fall.

Meanwhile back in Merrie England:
I listened to Radio Luxembourg on my new transistor radio,
made in Hong Kong, and managed to pass the 13+,
and read the Lion the Witch and the Wardrobe.
That year Elvis was King, Ah ha ha!
Elisabeth was Queen,
and Gay still meant cheerful and brightly coloured.

Welcome to the swinging sixties; some of my halcyon days,
Though it was oh so long ago it still seems like yesterday.

In 1962 the Russians shipped missiles to Cuba,
And the Yanks went to action stations,
As Khrushchev banged his shoe on the desk
defying the United Nations.
We held our breath as certain death
spelled the end of civilisation,
But President Kennedy saved the world
from nuclear annihilation.

So the world wasn't saved by a Bruce Willis,
Arnold Swarzenegger, John Wayne
or Superman type of character.
Well, Khrushchev was an erratic, vodka swilling, WW2 hero,
and Kennedy was allegedly a womaniser, having affairs with
Marilyn Monroe among others.
Perhaps the moral is that it's better to be a lover than a fighter;
If you want to save the world that is!

Welcome to the swinging sixties, some of my halcyon days,
Though it was oh so long ago, it still seems like yesterday.

In 1963 Valentina Tereshkova became the first woman in space,
And the Beatles 'Please, Please me' was released.
As Christine Keeler and Mandy Rice Davies
brought our government to its knees,
Bob Dylan told us the times are a-changin',
James Bond came from Russia with love,
And in November, in Dallas, John Kennedy
went to meet the angels above.

Meanwhile, I was in high school
wearing a school uniform 3 sizes too big.
You know - turn ups of industrial strength
on both the trousers and blazer.
In English Lit. I was reading a boring book
called Mr Polly by H. G. Wells;
Soon abandoned for The Gun by C S Forrester,
and Allan Quartermain by Rider Haggard.
When not studying English Lit. I read Lady Chatterley's Lover.
As a result I became so depraved
that I joined the Woodpecker darts team,
started smoking and drinking,
and completely forgot where I was
when Kennedy was assassinated.

Welcome to the swinging sixties, some of my halcyon days,
Though it was oh so long ago, it still seems like yesterday.

In 1964, this was the year all the oldies groaned,
Because they didn't understand the words
Sung by the Beatles and the Stones.
'The weekend starts here',
with Keith Fordyce and Cathy McGowan
on Ready, Steady, Go,
And all the in-crowd tuned in to Caroline on pirate radio.

Meanwhile, here in still Great Britain,
I could moo-oo-oo-oo-oove like Jagger,
James Bond was in Goldfinger,
and Shirley Bassey sang it.
Harold Wilson, yer darlin' 'Arold,
became Prime Minister.
He was obsessed with the pound in your pocket,
and the price of pipe tobacco.

My headmaster, Mr Harry told me
he didn't like my Beatles hairstyle,
And I said, "That's OK!" '
cause I didn't like what's was left of his hair.
He sent a letter home to my my mum about it,
And she wrote back saying she failed
to see how the length of my hair
could affect my academic ability.
I gave up smoking and soon after passed 10 GCE 'O' levels.
Mum was delighted, Mr Harry was outraged,
and then refused to present me with my certificates.

Welcome to the swinging sixties; some of my halcyon days,
Though it was oh so long ago it still seems like yesterday.

In 1965, on the only 3 TV channels;
still monochrome, comedy and satire were rife.
There was Not so Much a Programme more a Way of Life,
That was the Week that Was, better known as TW3,
And Not Only But Also with Peter Cook and cuddly Dudley.

Meanwhile, in a quiet world for Russians
the media discovered Mods and Rockers.
I went into the 6th form, got bored, bored, bored with it,
and discovered girls.
Janet Robinson was my first girlfriend.
Her dad ran the local chippie.
And 10 minutes of snogging with Janet Fishshop
as she was known,
Made you smell like last night's haddock and chips.
Oh Yeah! I gave up smoking again.
Took up eating fish and chips!

Welcome to the swinging sixties, some of my halcyon days,
Though it was oh so long ago, it still seems like yesterday.

In 1966, if you were a dedicated follower of fashion,
you bought your clothes in Carnaby Street.
The Monkees arrived on our TV's
as America's answer to the Beatles.
Mary Quant and Twiggy promoted the mini skirt.
The World Cup was in England,
and was won by players from West Ham,
and President Lyndon B Johnson delighted
in napalming Vietnam.

Meanwhile, I left School and started work in London;
bought a Lambretta scooter, and became a mod.
I had to leave school because by then
the uniform was 3 sizes too small.
Trousers, now turnupless (a new word)
were flapping round my knees,
and the sleeves on my blazer
were worn out at the elbows.
I got drunk for the first time in my life

the night after West Ham won the World Cup.
Good Excuse!
And girls discovered me.
Well! It was the era of the Mini skirt,
women's lib and burning bras,
and most important of all, deodorants for men.
Old Spice and Avon Spicy Mmm!

Welcome to the swinging sixties; some of my halcyon days,
Though it was oh so long ago it still seems like yesterday.

In 1967 it was all Waterloo sunsets
 in the summer of Love,
Jimi Hendrix and Purple Haze; hippies, and flower power,
and San Francisco filling those heady days.
Experiments with colour TV,
And the first heart transplants were underway,
And in a time of psychedelia
did anybody really see Emily play?

Meanwhile, it wasn't all good.
The Torrey Canyon spilled thousands of tons of oil
all over Cornwall's beaches,
and was bombed by the RAF.
I gave up smoking, and met, loved and lost Denise Frost,
my first serious girlfriend.
The Israelis had a 6-day war
and petrol prices rose to about 1/6 a gallon.
I tell you times were really hard!

I have to point out that after 50 years
I still don't know what a halcyon is?
And I'm convinced that if I ever found out,
I probably wouldn't be able to afford one!
That's actually a complete fib.
I looked it up,
and the halcyon is a mythical bird akin to a kingfisher.
So there!
Isn't education a wonderful thing?
And Wikipedia!

Welcome to the swinging sixties; some of my halcyon days,
Though it was oh so long ago it still seems like yesterday.

In 1968 it was the year of protest marches,
and we shall overcome,
Of CND, and Ban the Bomb, and anti-Vietnam.
Martin Luther King was inspired to have a dream,
and was then assassinated,
Dubcek gave the Czechoslovaks hope,
and so the Russians invaded.

Meanwhile, I bought this guitar,
and learned a few Bob Dylan songs;
spent most Sundays marching
from Trafalgar Square to Grosvenor Square,
watched Dad's Army and Doctor Who on the telly -
still not colour,
and drank loads of Watney's Red Barrel.
Apollo8 orbited the moon,
and I overcame the urge to give up smoking.

Yeah, about this halcyon business;
when I wrote this song I thought about
saying "salad days" instead.
But then, who wants to listen to songs about
lettuces, cucumbers and tomatoes?
That's not true either.
The expression "salad days"
is from Shakespeare's Antony and Cleopatra.
Let me quote!
"Salad days" is an idiomatic expression,
referring to a youthful time, accompanied by the inexperience,
enthusiasm, idealism, innocence, or indiscretion
that one associates with a young person.
That sounds a bit like me!

Welcome to the swinging sixties; some of my halcyon days,
Though it was oh so long ago it still seems like yesterday.

In 1969 we watched Apollo11 land upon the moon,
and Neil Armstrong's giant leap was the first,
But let's not forget, it also made Michael Collins
 the loneliest man in the Universe.
Bob Dylan came and played at the Isle of Wight,
Concorde took off for its maiden flight,
and John Cleese did those silly walks
on Monty Pythons Flying Circus.

Meanwhile, as the sixties drew to a close,
most public telephone boxes were vandalised,
the pubs still closed at half past ten,
and the 3 channels on TV started about 4
and finished about 11.
The only fast food restaurant was the Wimpy Bar.
All our pink bits on maps of the world began to disappear,

as all those ex-colonial countries renamed themselves,
usually with something starting with the letter Z,
and immediately started their civil war.
On the good side Roger Miller told us
that Engerland swings like a pendulum do?
What?
Oh! Never mind all that.
You could lay in a bed warmed by your electric blanket,
which you bought with your green shield stamps,
stare at the TV test card, or a fascinating lava lamp,
then wake up to a fresh cuppa
courtesy of your Goblin Teasmade,
which you bought with your Embassy coupons.
Such wealth, such decadence!
Oh! By the way, did I tell you, I gave up smoking again?

Goodbye to the swinging sixties; some of my salad days,
Though it was oh so long ago it still seems like yesterday.

CHAPTER 5
Aspire if you dare

"As I sit and practice my guitar,
I wonder if I'll get very far?"

I remember the Summer and You

The song "I remember the Summer and You" may be the very first poem that I ever wrote and kept, and it may have been written as early as 1965 or 66.

In 1965 I was going out with a girl called Janice Roseman, who lived in Walthamstow, and we were probably "together" for about 3 months. I met her one Sunday on a day trip to Walton on the Naze.

In 1966 I met a girl called Daphne, who rode a Triumph Tigercub motorbike, while I was on a week's holiday at Leysdown on the Isle of Sheppey. She came from Redhill in Surrey, and we wrote to each other for years. This poem was written for one of these two lovely ladies, and it became a song soon after I learned to play the guitar in 1968. I always imagined it was the sort of song that Cliff Richard might have sung, but it was never recorded?

Written circa 1965

Oh, I remember the summer;
the summer when I met you.
When I think of that summer,
and the things that we did do,
I know that in my life,
There is no one but you.

Oh, I remember the jukebox;
the songs I played for you,
the way I held you near me,
When bedtime was overdue;
the nights we danced together,
when the whole world was new.

Yes, I remember that summer
as the best that I have known,
when we walked on the sands together,
and we were all alone,
and as the leaves are falling now
we find our love had grown.

Yes, I remember the sunshine,
the sunshine in your eyes,
but I'll recall the tears,
the tears I couldn't cry,
after the summer was over,
when we said our goodbyes.

And, as I remember that summer
I never stop thinking of you,
and as long as I dream of that summer,
the thought of anyone new
makes me long for the last summer,
the summer when I met you.

Hermit Girl

By 1967 I had left school and started work, and had a Lambretta LD150 scooter. I had my first serious relationship with a girl called Denise who lived nearby in Hutton. I met her at her birthday party in February, and we were together until September 4th. The date is indelibly scratched on my memory, because after we broke up it took me a very long time to get over Denise. I suppose that she was my first love, and the hurt cut very deep. The inspiration for the song relates to two things. The first is that she always sat in her bedroom window looking out at the world going by on Rayleigh Road, in Hutton near Brentwood. The second is that there are elements of the structure and tone that follow the lyric to the song "Suzanne" by Leonard Cohen.

Written October 1967

She sits there in her room, and stares down at the world,
I know that she is lonely, the lovely hermit girl,
and faceless people passing by don't realise she's there;
the pitiless don't hear her sigh, don't see her long dark hair,
and I want to go to see her, and I want to ease her mind,
do what I can to please her,
and catch the sparkle of her eyes moving into mine.

She sparkles every day down to the street below,
and I've got to find a way for my concern to show.
The lovely hermit girl, silent through the window,
floating on the breeze, and weeping as the sun goes,
swaying on a rainbow, and crying at the moon.
And I'm sure that she is lonely, and I'm certain she is sad,
and I want to go to see her, and I want to ease her mind,
do what I can to please her,
and catch the teardrops from her eyes moving into mine.

The summer now lies fallen, white crispness fills the air;
the hermit girl lies broken, for she is not aware,
that I want to break her sorrow, and hold her tiny hand,
give her a new tomorrow, and make her understand,
that life behind the sunset is simpler than outside it,
And life inside a trumpet is better when you hide it.
And I want to go to see her; the lovely hermit girl,
do what I can to please her; break the eternal spell,
and catch the laughter of her eyes moving into mine.

Dedication

This is another piece about my first love Denise showing just how much that 18 year old virgin was smitten with the lovely young lady. It's a bit too sentimental really, and reads like something off a birthday card. What do you think?

Written circa 1967

We have our times and times,
they are both good and bad,
but when I stop and think sometimes,
I am so very glad.

The times we are together
I treasure very much,
I kiss her lips, caress her hair,
and shiver at her touch.

She is the very world to me,
and every breath I take;
together we'll be forever,
and her my life I'll make.

Sometimes she may be cruel to me,
but I place her high above,
I love her more than all the world -
She is the girl I love.

But I am, and but I can

After Denise I spiralled downwards into gloom and doom, and it didn't leave me for many years. Hence the interest in "slash your wrists" music like that on Leonard Cohen's album "Songs from a Room". Most of the things I wrote then had a heavy tone. This is just one of them.

Written circa 1968

I am blind, but I can see,
I am deaf, but I can hear,
I am dumb, but I can speak,
I am normal, but I'm a freak.

I am rash, but I am wise,
I am illiterate, but I can read,
I am a cripple, but I can walk,
I have no conversation, but I can talk.

I am dark, but I am light,
I am day, but I am night,
I can't fly, but I've taken flight,
I am weak, but I can fight,
I am heavy, but I am light,
I am in love, but I am in hate,
I am patient, but I can't wait.

I'm looking at the ground,
But I see the sky,
I am alive,
But I want to die.

Why I don't know what it is

From an emotional point of view the year 1968 wasn't a good one for me, and I spent most of my time down in the mouth, and utterly miserable. This is another "I'm feeling very sorry for myself, and nobody cares." piece of writing from my suicide period.

Written circa 1968

Why is the night dark?
Why is he day light?
Why is the sky blue?
Why is is the grass green?
Why? Oh, why?

Why does a dog bark?
Why has a hill height?
Why does a quiz have a clue?
Why is invisible unseen?
Why? Oh, why?

I don't know why, or who, or where, or when, or which, or how -
I don't know anything right now.

I know one thing that's near to me,
I know someone who's dear to me,
But why is it not clear to me?

I don't know why, but I know who,
Or at least, I think I do.

I don't know why the sun doesn't shine,
I don't know where or when in time,
I don't know which, so few and many,
I don't know how, there isn't any.

But I know one thing, of that I'm sure,
It's probably, most definitely, possibly, certain,
I think.

Aspire if you dare

At the same party where I met Denise in 1967 I met a neighbour called Barry. We became inseparable friends with the same musical interests, especially with regard to Bob Dylan and Roy Harper. We went to many music events together including the Cambridge Folk Festival, the Isle of Wight Festival in 1969, and the Weeley Festival in 1971, and we were regulars at the Les Cousins Folk Club in Greek Street, Soho. I learned my first guitar chords from Barry, and he was with me when I bought my lifelong friend - an Eko Ranger 12 Guitar, at Rose Morris in Shaftesbury Avenue in 1968. The short doodle was written then.

Written circa 1968

As I sit and practice my guitar
I wonder if I'll get very far,
or shall I leave things
just the way they are?
Or maybe play the harmonica,
or be very clever,
and play them both together.
Yes, and with a cymbal on each knee,
or maybe not,
We'll see.

Stood up Blues

Around this time, through my best friend Barry, I began to develop more than a casual interest in musical genres like Bob Dylan, Roy Harper, and in particular in blues formats. There was a thriving folk and blues scene in most half decent pubs in the late 60's, and the frequent visits to the famous Les Cousins all night basement club in Greek Street in Soho included performances by Alexis Korner, Bert Jansch and John Renbourn and many up and coming blues players. This piece is quite a simple blues example which fits easily into a 12 bar format. It was never recorded.

Written 22nd June, 1968

Light up another cigarette,
pour out another glass of beer,
It's getting close to 9 o'clock,
and soon she will be here.

Maybe I've been stood up,
I don't think that's fair;
The time now is nearly 9,
why doesn't she appear?

The room is getting hazy,
my eyes are failing to see clear,
It's a long time now since 9 o'clock,
And still she hasn't got here.

I suppose she's found someone else,
and going to I don't know where,
Our time to meet went long ago,
And still she hasn't appeared.

Suppose I'd better give up now,
After I've finished my beer,
Wow, just in time, she's made it,
So glad at last she's here.

Absolutely Crumpled

I found this bit of scribble amongst a lot of handwritten bits and pieces. What it relates to I have no idea, but it does seem to have some poetic merit?

Written 1969ish

The sun has cast its watery rays upon the broken ground,
a mask of hate is sitting there with trumpets all around -
my eyes are hidden in my hands,
I fear no word or sound,
except the moaning of the wind
echoing through the sky,
And messages of sympathy that come from passers-by.

Musical Differences in Arthur's Band

This little story was probably written under the influence of some waccy baccy. Unlike most of my friends I never dabbled in drugs any further than the occasional cannabis spliff, whereas many of my gang went on to try speed and LSD. That just wasn't for me. The circles I moved in included many friends who were very capable at playing guitar, bass, keyboard or drums. It was a time when being able to fingerpick a well known tune like "Streets of London" was almost a badge of honour.

Written circa 1969

Cast of Characters:
Harry the haystack, the drummer
Arthur the magic apple barrel, the lead guitarist
Cecil the psychedelic carrot, the bass guitarist
Glib the giant tongue, the singer
Victoria and Penelope, the amazing glow worm sisters, the backing singers
Mrs Egotits, the bosom woman, the dancer

Arthur took a deep breath, raised himself up to his full cooperage, and spectacularly smashed out the last E-major chord on his beaten-up old guitar. There was a brief pause, and then the whole arena erupted with applause and high acclaim.

Cecil was a special carrot, not just an ordinary orange-coloured, parsley-topped type, he was psychedelic, which meant that when Arthur played Cecil flipped, and everybody knew it. Years of addiction to D.D.T. had seen to that. So Cecil flipped as expected, and then flopped exhausted, in the shade of Glib the giant tongue, who was shouting, "More! More!" at the top of his voice, and spraying everyone with saliva.

Everybody else was cool. It wasn't that they weren't excited about Arthur's performance, they were excited sure enough, but their enthusiasm had been somewhat dampened by Glib's antics.

"Hey! Cut that out man", said Harry to Glib, "Cool it, or I'll smother you."

Glib stuck himself out at Harry, and Harry retaliated by throwing a bale at him.

"Hey! You don't know what happens to damp haystacks, do you?" shouted Harry in exasperation, "Well, I'll tell you man, internal combustion, that's what and ....."

He was cut off by Arthur, who, as usual, was threatening to leave the band if things didn't calm down.

"Cool it! Or else I'm splitting." he shouted.

After another couple of minutes, when Penelope and Victoria had stopped screaming, and some sense of order was restored, Arthur began the next song...

Stratford Junction Blues

The words to this song were written while myself and Barry were waiting on the platform of Stratford Station for a very late (or was it very early?) train into London. They fit perfectly into the Eric Clapton instrumental called "Slowhand". They were recorded the next day on a Vortexion reel to reel tape recorder in Barry's bedroom. The recording has since been lost.

Our gang had lots of discussions about who was the best guitarist in the world. There were many nominations, including Eric Clapton, Jimmy Page, Ritchie Blackmore, and Jimi Hendrix, and a local lad whom we all knew as Johnny Aldridge.

Written with help from Barry Childs, circa 1969

Here I am waitin' on Stratford Junction,
and it's 3' o'clock in the morn.
The lines are quiet,
the train's not comin',
and everybody has long gone.

I'm waitin' here on Stratford Junction,
with one cold, black, stray cat.
A young girl's waitin,
Sittin' nearby,
And I turn around, and give her the eye.

The train ain't a-comin' for sometime yet,
rattling its way along the track,
I'm cold and tired,
on Stratford Junction,
but I'm not goin' to turn back.

What did it mean to you that I was cold and tired on the station?
You didn't even know that I was there.
Come on, why didn't you listen to me?
I want to come home to you.

OK, Baby, I'm comin' back to you,
I still want to be with you,
and here I am waitin' for the train,
to take me to St John's Wood,
It's three o'clock in the early morning,
And I'm cold.

Canine Thought

Sometimes there is just a quick philosophical thought.

Written circa 1969

A home without a dog,
Is like a dog without a home.

Frederic's Fanatical Left Wing Song

The years 1968 to 1972 were the heyday of the weekend hippie. Sundays at the demonstration in Trafalgar Square, CND - Ban the Bomb, We shall overcome, Yanks out of Vietnam, were de rigueur. Who cared about the politics? Be there or be square. Here is the first of two little ditties capturing the essence of the time for me.

Written circa 1969

I think it may be true to say
that in Trafalgar Square today
without a doubt, but with dismay,
from the banners held in bright array
the favourite colour is red.

But it also may be true to say
that all the pigeons have flown away,
and poor Nelson - he is dead.
So we'll sing this song as we march ahead.

Keep that banner floating Frederic,
keep that ensign high,
hold that banner proudly Frederic,
flying in the sky.

I'll tell you now, but not in jest,
the fountains spray of opal mist
falls on no ground the sun has kissed,
but on the faces of those who list'
to the speaker's words of lace,
as I'll tell you now, but not in jest
that he's brainwashing you to do your best
for the Internationale to unite the human race.
So we'll sing this song as we make our pace.

Keep that banner floating Frederic,
keep that ensign high,
hold that banner proudly Frederic,
flying in the sky.

Susie's Square

And here is the second ditty inspired during the '68 to '72 protest march period. Susie was real, not imagined, but her intervention in my life was only short and sweet.

Written circa 1969

'T'was not for politics, but for fun
that I did go to Trafalgar Square,
and as I sighted Nelson's stand
I joined the demonstration there.
While crossing to the battleground
I spied a friend, whose face was rare,
who stood among her comrades there,
ready to march to Grosvenor Square.

Susie, Susie, came to the square
where the lions are tame,
and the tigers are spare,
Susie, Susie, saw her there;
Saw you in the square, little Susie.

'T'was not for politics, but for fun
that I marched with them to the embassy,
and as we chanted arm in arm
I met a young girl called Susie.
She spoke very soft, and her eyes were brown,
she was five feet two, and pretty,
and after passing the embassy,
I lost her in Hyde Park. What a pity!

Susie, Susie, came to the square
where the lions are tame,
and the tigers are spare,
Susie, Susie, lost you there;
Lost you in the square, little Susie.

Juvenile Delicatessen

You'll need a translation for this, because I've no idea what it means either!
Sometimes words came in short spurts and unintelligible formations.

Written circa 1969

Spotted Dalmatian, cum-Alsatian,
Canine member of the human race,
looks in the mirror through the eyes in the back of his tail,
and sees his face.

Black and gold, moonshine madly,
Twin carburettor, six cylinder,
Chauffeur-driven, single-seater,
Ford - Mercedes - Benz drones by,
Off!
To Eldorado, in the sky.

CHAPTER 6

It Happens to the Best of us
"Further research reveals that
walls also have ice-cream."

Here are some more extracts from the unpublished book "Taking Chances, Making Choices". This time it covers the period from 1970 to 1980.

Taking Chances, Making Choices

CHAPTER 6

Settling Down to Married Life - A canter through my life 1970 onwards

Upon the tightrope line

As independent travellers Barry and I had been around a bit, and had a great time, but the following year we went travelling again. This time we kept our jobs, and merely took the 2 week summer vacation that was all that employers gave in 1970. We planned to go on a Cosmos coach tour of central European capitals; Berlin, Prague, Vienna and Budapest. All the main venues were spectacular and exciting to visit, but some unexpected and incredible eye openers were in store. Travel broadens the mind for sure, but it can also cut at the soul.

Berlin, and particularly the Kurfürstendamm at night, started a 2 week long booze party with absolutely no let up. Prague was swarming with the olive green uniforms of Russian soldiers, but there weren't any tanks or military activity other than at the border with Austria, and beer was 4 old pence a pint. It tasted like a dog's wet coat smells, but there is no bad beer!

Vienna, apart from the Big Wheel in Prater Park was just any old imperial city, but with an incredibly lively and heady nightlife sponsored by an alluring cocktail of new wine and the music of Strauss.

In Budapest we stayed at the Hotel Beke which had a night club visited by the Hungarian Politburo. We then visited Lake Balaton; and I discovered that in that poor, underdeveloped, and oppressed country little old me, with my limited financial status, was an immensely rich man. Nothing was out of my grasp.

However, my abiding memory of this trip is of none of these fine cities, but of something with a sadness, overpowering and immovable, as if there was a permanent stain of blackness and gloom. This cloud hung over the East

German City of Dresden. A main street of sorts had been rebuilt, with a huge department store fronted by massive and empty plate glass windows, and there were seemingly endless rows of bland, identical worker's apartments. Surrounding this modern rebuilt area were what was left of this city after the bombing raids of World War 2. Churches and galleries and other outstanding ancient structures had been all left in ruins, all unrestored and abandoned as monuments to the atrocities of war. If there was any equivalent of Hiroshima in Europe, I have no doubt that Dresden filled this awful void. Perhaps it had something to do with the unrelenting drizzling rain, but there was an aura of stillness, timelessness about it, like it was just a photograph, a fragment of some magnum opus, which had gone disastrously wrong.

As the coach left, a choking lump nestled in my throat, a sense of deadening numbness crept into my body, and I was filled will an urge to quickly be whisked somewhere else.

Giant leaps

My job as a Sales Correspondent for Phillips Petroleum was interesting enough, in that I now imported, warehoused, and re-distributed rubber, plastic and other chemical petroleum bi-products in the UK. But there were 3 managers, 3 secretaries, and just my old mucker, Brian Chamberlain from Gallenkamp and myself doing the work.

Labelled the unwanted section because of our top heavy jobs-for-the-boys structure, we made 4 moves of our office location within Portland House within 1 year. Then in 1970 some rationalisation of staff was deemed necessary. The outcome of this was that one manager lost his job, one was re-deployed, 2 secretaries were re-assigned, and I became surplus to requirements. I was called into the remaining manager's office one day in July and advised

"Thanks for creating order from our chaos, but we don't need you any more."

Within a few years I had managed to go on the dole, and then be made redundant, and both before they became fashionable.

After discussion, Philips agreed to re-deploy me. I spent 4 months twiddling my thumbs, and getting pissed at the expense of any warehouse or shipping organisation that was willing to throw business lunches at me. In November the personnel section accused me of not trying to get another position, (true), and sent me reluctantly for an aptitude test to join the computer department. This simple logic and number progressions test was a breeze, and I was then obliged to attend an interview with the Data Processing Manager, John Holman.

He was 25, and he had a dark blue suit and short hair, and his office was the size of a large broom cupboard. He sat behind his desk at my interview, put his hands behind his head, and his feet on his desk, and enquired of me,

"Can you tell me why you want this job, and why I should select you for it?"

I put my hands behind my head, put my feet up on the other side of his desk, and retorted, "Well, John, I don't want this job!"

A week later I started as a trainee computer operator on a 2 shift (mornings and evenings) system. I was working on a thoroughly modern IBM 360/20 card based 16k memory computer. The discovery that in the DP department they tolerated, casual clothing, long hair and a more cavalier attitude generally appealed immensely; and it wasn't too long before I realised that this accidental change of career suited me like a foot in a sock. I had made my giant leap just over a year after Neil Armstrong!

In 1971 the computer department was coping with the difficulties of the UK economy transferring to decimal coinage, and with a regular and steadily increasing income I started to learn to drive...

Hair again

Times had changed, and within a few short years, there was another hair-related incident in 1971 while I was at Phillips Petroleum. By this time my hair was at its greatest ever length; so long I could tuck it under my armpits and still touch ends together in the middle of my back. John Holman called me to his office, and began as casually as usual, with his feet on the desk, by saying, "Mick, we've got a problem. Next week we're getting a visit from Jolly Backer. He's one of those redneck vice presidents of Phillips 66 from Bartlesville, Oklahoma."

I smiled and John continued.

"So, here's the deal," he explained, "Either get your hair cut, or go on nights for a week."

"Thanks John," I responded, getting up to leave, "I'll go on nights"...

Rocking and rolling

My favourite band through the 60's and early 70's, after many short unfaithful diversions to other mostly one-hit wonders, was still the Rolling Stones. I still bought every one of their albums on vinyl including the re-issued hits and misses collections issued in revenge by Decca after the band's less than friendly defection to form their own label. But eventually I outgrew them, and their music started to turn away from their bluesy roots, towards more soulful or anti-blues directions, and that is when I threw in the towel.

As the music scene continued to develop away from sugary love pleas and romantic ballads of the 50's and 60's, and with the Stones losing that raw edge to their sound, there were numerous exciting musical directions and possibilities, spawning brilliant inventive live performances. A new musicality and professionalism blossoming out of the blues background, took possession of the musical reins, and in 70/72 heavy rock, or progressive rock as it was sometimes called, emerged. Allegiance was swapped to the more powerful driving "heavy" rock of Led Zeppelin, Deep Purple, Black Sabbath, Wishbone Ash, and the spacey " I've already left that planet far behind!" music and pyrotechnics of Pink Floyd (pre Dark Side of the Moon). I also travelled into space and other dimensions many times with the chants and anthems of the enigmatic space cowboys known as Hawkwind...

Several more giant leaps

In 1974 I bought my first decent car; a 1969, 1600L Ford Capri, and in early April, as if fate was playing all the aces, on my first trip to Wales in the Capri, I met Rosemary, the girl who was to become my wife. We met in a pub in Hereford called the Grapes on 27th April, went on holiday together camping in the Elan Valley in June, and by July Rosemary had moved into my family home in Brentwood. Within a month, we had our own home in a caravan in Noak Hill, Harold Hill. We had 2 of everything; chairs, plates, forks, knives, spoons, cups, all borrowed, and no telly. In true whirlwind romance style we were married at Malvern Register Office on 7th December, 1974. Unlike most men I can easily remember my wedding anniversary; I always used to say, "It's easy! We were married on the same day as the Japanese bombed Pearl Harbour!"

Living in the caravan was hard! There was no bath, cramped living conditions, and in the winter the coal-based heating was either blast furnace when on, or Antarctica when off. All our clothes went mildew in the small wardrobe, and we had to keep clean by either going to the swimming baths or visiting my mum's once a week...

Contented

In May 1975, in a boozy haze, on my brother-in-law, Brian's large colour telly, the "good year for me" trend continued, when I watched excited and bursting with pride, as West Ham beat a Fulham side including the ultimate Hammers hero, Bobby Moore, 2-0 in the FA Cup Final.

In September I changed my employment to work for the City of Westminster Council. They had recently acquired a Sperry mainframe computer. A slightly higher salary was negated by a more expensive and less convenient journey from our future home in East Tilbury. After the pleasure of seeing our new home through all the building stages we moved in on 20th December 1975; a bitterly cold day. We had acquired some cheap furniture and a full sized double bed. The one in the caravan was the pull-out-of-the-wall type, three quarter size, and in the last few days we had begun to burn some of the wood in its construction to keep warm. The best thing, which added to the comforting and contented glow of our first proper brand new home, just before Xmas, was the 3 kilowatt 3 bar electric fire in the lounge. It did not matter that we had no carpet, and sat on an Indian rug, a present from my mum, to enjoy this welcome luxury. It did not matter that there was no heating elsewhere in the flat, and getting up out of bed still involved enduring freezing breath, frost on the inside of the windows, and cold floors. We had a new home, which we could just about manage to afford.

It ain't half hot, Dad!

Less than a month after our move Rosemary provided me with the biggest shock of my life when she announced that she was pregnant. Despite the difficulties that the unexpected start to our family would inevitably present we approached this news with joy and eager anticipation.1976 would be another blistering hot summer, another record breaking best ever, and Rosemary needed to work up till July, to make the smallest possible dent in our financial situation...

Michelle was born in the Maternity Unit of Orsett hospital at about 7 p.m. on September 12th after Rosemary had apparently been 2 weeks late, and needed to be induced. I was present throughout the birth, offering encouragement, mopping Rosemary's brow, holding her hand, and with tears in my eyes and a lump in my throat watched Michelle arrive. Some hours later, at home in front of the telly, I felt strangely detached and isolated from the day's previous events; as if it had all been a fantasy.

One win, one draw?

The world's most powerful man in 1978 was a former peanut farmer, US President Jimmy Carter, who "brokered" the peace treaty between Sadat of Egypt and Begin of Israel, resulting in them being awarded the Nobel peace prize.

After many years of protests throughout the "civilised" world, and after the much welcomed end of LBJ's presidential term, by which time the overall "Nam" death toll had risen to 45,600, Jimmy Carter abandoned the paranoid domino theory in Southeast Asia and pulled out with a dishonourable draw, after a cease-fire on 28th January 1973.

Yuppies and Ayatollahs

Back at Westminster things were changing as I became a member of the new Operations Support Group in 1979, and Mrs Thatcher arrived as Britain's first woman Prime Minister. She was arrogant and over confident, and had shown her true metal at a lower level by attaining the label, "milk snatcher Thatcher" in a previous Tory administration. Ultimately though, she would be lucky enough to get all the breaks.

The whole country appeared fed up with the inept, union dominated, Labour government, and yearned for a new direction, which the Iron Lady promised to provide in no uncertain terms.

When she took office, nobody could know that Mrs Thatcher would be privileged to focus the nation's pride and sense of international justice through the Falklands War. After the "Argies" invaded, following threatening postures early in 1982, for perhaps the final time in history, Britannia briefly ruled the waves again. But in truth the enemy's leadership, General Galtieri and his cronies, miscalculated the reaction of the British people to protect

their friends from 7000 miles and 3 week's sailing time away. The "Argies" were doomed to failure the moment our naval task force set sail on 5th April. Besides which, they were ill equipped and badly led, borne out by their short-lived occupation of Port Stanley, and unconditional surrender there on 14th June, only a few weeks later.

Mrs Thatcher's other fortuitous ace, was that she arrived just before the beginning of the technology revolution that saw personal computing come to everybody's desk as an essential element of their daily lives. This became the factor most instrumental in creating and promoting the get-rich-quick Yuppie culture…

Triumph and tragedy

Michelle had soon grown into a toddler, and Rosemary wanted a home with a garden, and so after placing a deposit on a new house in Chelmsford in July 1979, we once again enjoyed the pleasure of seeing our home built. We moved on 15th February 1980; finances stretched to the limit again, with the full expectation that the old saying "New home, new baby" would arise a second time…

CHAPTER 7
Ain't it a Shame?
***"And all that we have done today
is toll the bell of doom."***

Ain't it a shame?
(Wake up Senator)
(The new American National Anthem)

Perhaps it was inevitable after all those marches to Grosvenor Square that it would be natural to have a bone to pick with America in general and Americans in particular. So this is a protest song that was never recorded.

Written circa 1970

American nation you're in disgrace,
spreading pollution through the human race,
leading exploration of outer space,
filling up our oceans with atomic waste.
And it's a shame!
Sure is a shame!
Ain't it a shame the Americans came
and culled the Indian Race?

The almighty dollar rides no more,
wasted away by conflict and war;
now you're licking your battle sores.
They're nailing up the White House doors.
And it's a shame?
Sure is a shame!
Ain't it a shame the Americans came
and killed the Indian squaws?

Ghetto children in the Summertime
playing in the streets of crime;
and Senator Buddy can you spare a dime,
or find the time to clean the grime?
And it's a shame!
Sure it a shame!
Ain't it a shame the Americans came
and stopped the redskin line?

The star strangled banner is being torn down.
Your New York skies are turning brown.
Your rat-faced senator's wearing a frown,
while President Clown is wearing the crown.
And it's a shame!
Sure is a shame!
Ain't it a shame the Americans came
and mowed the Indians down?

Success story

If someone learns to play the guitar and wants to write songs, then one day they're going to write something cynical like this about how difficult it might be to become an overnight success, and maybe how you'd feel if you ever got there.
Written circa 1970

Wandering down the road, a guitar over his shoulder,
maybe he's nineteen; maybe he's a bit older,
beat up jeans, torn up shirt,
can't see his face, under the dirt,
Man! He doesn't care, and he doesn't work -
but he's as free as you or me
to be anything he wants to be.

Played to the people who passed by in the street;
spent most of the day standing on his feet.
One rainy day he's doing his best;
Man said son just take a little rest,
I'm gonna sign you up right now for world wide success -
and you'll be as free as anybody
to be anything you want to be.

Now he tops the Bill on the music shows;
a name and a face that everybody knows.
Bought himself a penthouse suite,
runs four cars and dresses neat,
He earns ten thousand pounds every week.
And he's as free as you or me
to be anything he wants to be.

Doesn't have the time to recall his past.
He's enjoying his money while his money lasts.
Sings and plays; plays and sings,
parties, girls, and diamond rings -
He's got happy days; he's got pretty things -
But he's not free like you or me
to be anything he wants to be.

The Wall

I had first hand experience of the Berlin Wall, and its cruel implications for innocent German people on both sides of the divide. In addition, as I explained earlier regarding the cloud that hung over Dresden, I sensed the oppressive nature of a divide and rule political doctrine that required walls for its enforcement. Here's yet another song that was never recorded. Note carefully that my "The Wall" was written some 9 years before Pink Floyd recorded a very successful album with the same name.
Written circa 1970

The children of the revolution
have marched along their streets;
No basis to their constitution,
No shoes upon their feet;
Yet they were all so happy, there in their people's lands,
They knew about democracy; it joins the people's hands.

For East is East and West is West,
and ne'er the twain shall meet,
And one has more and one has less,
And neither sees defeat;
And yet they're all so happy in their promised lands,
They know about democracy, there in the people's band.

They threw a wall around them all
to keep them on their side,
And they weren't allowed to wave to the folks
who lived on the other side;
Because they're all so happy, there in their paradise,
They could not see democracy through the other people's eyes.

This was the wall of death we know;
and many people died;
where many sons have lost their breath,
and many mothers cried;
And they were all so happy in their people's lands,
They knew about democracy - cut of the people's hands.

It was a sore point to us all -
could've started World War Three,
but would we win because we knew
about democracy,
Would we have won because we knew that our side was the good,
and left nothing there but barren sands where once the people stood?

Thinking in the Key of D

Cat Stevens' song "Where do the Children Play?" was probably part of the influence for this little poem. A retrospective look at the words fixes the sentiment firmly in the early 70's

Written circa 1970

In the bleak city street stands a freak,
and he reeks of the weed,
with him is his lady, soon to have a baby,
maybe it came from his seed.
See the world has passed them by,
see the shadows in their eyes,
hear them yield a sigh before they say,
Hey, this world your building,
Is it safe for my children?
Will it be a good place to play?

In the pool at the school teacher rules
from a stool on the ledge.
No-one points to the joints in the methods she appoints;
anointed at the edge.
Deep beneath maternal smiles
thoughts stretch out eternal miles;
pausing for a while before she says,
Hey, this world your building,
Is it safe for my children?
Will it be a good place to play?

Stand by for a Centipede

Well, up to now you probably thought Edward Lear wrote pretty good nonsense poetry with "The Owl and the Pussycat" among others. But this is absolute nonsense of a very different sort. There's lots of name dropping and topical references to people and events from the 1970's, which might fling you back to a forgotten era in your own time machine.

Written circa 1970

Sweet memories of prostate glands,
and rotting Coca-Cola cans,
aid inspection and detection for vivisection plans,
for an over-sexed cornflake box,
and ten pairs of L.B.J.'s socks,
while Mao Sae Tung is in the stocks,
and Ho Chi Minh, the cunning fox,
is painted from head to toe
in the blood of Edgar Alan Poe,
because he didn't know
who was sleeping with his wife.

Gentle throbbings of a caterpillar's nose
forced Harold Wilson to remove his clothes,
in anticipation of legislation for nationalisation ideas,
on the underground airlines,
where you'll find Liberace's wines,
are in quarantine for signs,
of General de Gaulle's underpants,
since he lost them in a dance
 with all the prostitutes in France,
and Ho Chi Minh's made no advance
 in his investigations.

Now, Mary Queen of Scots wants to know
why she let her knickers go,
in acceptance or expectance for descendance plans,
for unofficial tea-breaks at Number Ten,
where Kosygin like a hen,
puts his teeth back in again,
to go to bed with Sophia Loren,
under the fountains in Trafalgar Square,
where Sandie Shaw and Yogi Bear,
make love on a cheese and tomato sandwich,
and don't care who Ho Chi Minh is.

Then Lord Snowdon in his Ascot suit
laughs and gives Rasmus the boot,
for entertaining and displaying discriminating blacks,
in Fred's cafe on the main road east,
where Tom and Jerry play beauty and the beast,
and Cassius Clay speaks like a priest;
Mohammed Ali's sporting life has ceased,
and the busty beauties try no more to get their statistics through the door
because Ho Chi Minh is on the floor bathing in tomato ketchup.

Bell of doom

To use a quote from a Freddy Mercury song this was written by someone who "Grew up tall and proud, under the shadow of a mushroom cloud." It was a time in history where the threat of global warfare and nuclear oblivion were real and not imagined fears. The eco warriors were on their first faltering sorties into the hearts and minds of planet Earth dwellers, and comparing the creation of our natural world with the best that mankind could muster was a growing phenomena.

Over the next few years, I suppose that Black Sabbath's doomy lyrics echoed this paranoia best of all. Just for example take a listen to their brilliant song "War Pigs".

Written circa 1970

Upon the wings of a bird is borne
the wrath of grey raging skies.
The green leaves from the trees are torn
by the savage butterfly.
The honeybee steals sweetness from
the mouths of the summer blooms;
and man has produced an atom bomb
to toll the bell of doom.

The big cat king of the jungle roars
and pounces upon his prey.
The cruel sea crashes upon the shores
and sweeps the land away.
The warmth of the summer night is gone
and cold weaves winter's loom;
and man has produced an atom bomb
to toll the bell of doom.

My lady sleeps so silently;
like a softly cooing dove,
but now she comes to waken me,
and bring me all her love.
My lady has my fine strong son
alive within her womb;
and man has produced an atom bomb
to toll the bell of doom.

Bell of doom

Twenty years later we knew all about global warming, climate change, and how our continuing exploitation of the Earth's resources was affecting the potential longevity of our existence on our planet. It's pretty sad that we still haven't really done that much about it a further 25 years on. My poetical constructions are, I would like to think, less crude, and the "punch line" is somewhat mellowed by the time this rewrite comes along.

Rewritten and amended circa 1990

Upon frail wings of a bird is borne
cruel wrath of grey, raging skies,
and green leaves from lean trees are torn
by savage butterflies,
while freedom bees steal secret sweetness
from cool summer blooms,
and all that they have done today
is toll the bell of doom.

Wild, big cat, king of the jungle roars
and pounces to kill his prey.
Storm lashed seas crash along the shores
to sweep deep sands away.
Fresh warmth of damp summer nights so long
Till cold weaves winter's loom,
and all that they have done today
is toll the bell of doom.

It Happens to the Best of Us

Listening to far too much Leonard Cohen music is probably the trigger for writing little philosophical tip-bits like this?

Written circa 1971

By the time I reach Heaven
I will probably be dead.
So will you,
Ha! Ha!

Blood on the Breeze

Perhaps I was lucky enough to be born too late for conscription, and consequently I've never served in an army or been to war. So, on first analysis I have no right to come up with stuff like this. But by 1971 I'd listened to an awful lot of protest songs especially by Bob Dylan, and it's possible that the inspiration for this never recorded song was his "Masters of War". Funny, I do believe that Mr Zimmerman never served in the armed forces either. That's enough of a validation for me.

Written circa 1971

Have you ever seen the men who put this rifle in my hands
to march the dusty roads in many far off lands,
and willingly to take another man's life,
with the blast of a gun, or the blade of a knife?
We're keeping the peace in the dens of the foe -
Well, when they're end comes, I hope they die slow.

Have you ever seen the men who build the big bombs
to protect and defend us from communist bonds,
so that all men can strive for the sake of world peace;
So that hunger, and murder, and suffering will cease?
Well, they're down in their chamber with loyalty true;
counting their money, and counting on you.

Have you ever seen the men who made this nightmare?
Have they seen the gassed children screaming for air,
and the broken body of the refugee,
Starving on his feet as he stares at me?
The wells are all dry, and the earth it is parched.
Tell me how many miles, have they ever marched?

How many of these men smell the blood on the breeze,
taste the bitterness of hate; hear no sounds in the trees;
but the roar of the guns, and the bombs in the skies,
and an ear bursting scream as another man dies?
If I ever go home I'll shout it so clear
that it should have been them and not me. that was here.

God Bless Our Mother

This song is going back to the same worries expressed in "The Wall"
earlier. This time I'm telling a story about Mother Russia's need to put
what Hitler cutely termed "lebensraum" in between the Soviet lands and
those of the supposed enemy in the shape of oppressed communist
satellites. What happens then repeatedly whenever the mother's children
are naughty? I suppose it's pretty natural to worry about these sorts of
things when you're young and think you can change the world.

Written circa 1971

Mother Russia had to hush
a naughty child of hers;
so the Kremlin ogres rumbled out
from the Katyn forest firs,
And travelled swiftly southward
to where influence had waned,
to Budapest, where it saw best
that terror should now reign.

And red, red, red, ran the blood that they shed,
And red, red, red, the flag that they carry is red.

The Magyars fought with bricks and stones
against grenades and tanks,
and blood and thunder echoed out
along the Danube's banks.
David met Goliath,
but alas his sling was slack -
The giant clenched an iron fist
and broke poor David's back.

And red, red, red, ran the blood that they shed,
And red, red, red, the flag that they carry is red.

The Warsaw pact was still intact;
the shadow still hung red;
the children of the revolution
slept in Mother's bed.
In a square in Prague
where Wenceslas had stood
Alexander Dubcek
wasn't being good.

And red, red, red, ran the blood that they shed,
And red, red, red, the flag that they carry is red.

The ogres rumbled out again
from within their hideaway -
A thousand tanks would stop the pranks
these naughty children played.
A ruthless coup was carried through,
a hideous rape they say;
and centuries old Bohemian kings
wept in their graves that day.

And red, red, red, ran the blood that they shed,
And red, red, red, the flag that they carry is red.

A tiny child in East Berlin
Despairingly, did say,
"Why did they build that great big wall
where I once used to play?
And why does Mother come along
and take our toys away?
And why does Mother come along
and take our toys away?

And red, red, red, ran the blood that they shed,
And red, red, red, the flag that they carry is red.

Distance from the day

This is simpler less worrying stuff. A song with a nice little chorus.

Written circa 1971

The dawn it breaks across the blue lake;
the morning wakens before long,
in every tree, Nature's symphony
greets the new morning with a song.

I am all, I am so small,
I often lose my way,
Beneath the shrouds, the tortured crowds,
The distance from the day.

The sun has shone, the summer's gone,
I walk along a windy mile,
Up in the sky, geese flying high,
Going down South for a while.

I am all, I am so small,
I often lose my way,
Beneath the shrouds, the tortured crowds,
The distance from the day.

The world turns round, the sun goes down,
here is the end of another day.
The spell is cast, the night falls fast,
The gulls wing out across the bay.

I am all, I am so small,
I often lose my way,
Beneath the shrouds, the tortured crowds,
The distance from the day.

Some distance from the day

Again, about 20 years later I come up with what I hope is more poetical, softer rewrite, and then eventually after another 10 years or so (in May 2001) I recorded it at Amber Studios on the demo album "Never Enough".

Rewritten and amended circa 1991

Cold dawn it breaks, 'cross the blue lake,
New morning wakens before long,
In every tree there's a symphony,
Greets breaking morning with a song.

I am all, I am so small,
I often lose my way,
Among dark clouds, or tortured crowds,
Some distance from the day.

Warm sun has shone, last summer's gone,
I walk along a windy mile,
Up in the sky, geese flying high,
Going down South for a while.

I am all, I am so small,
I often lose my way,
Among dark clouds, or tortured crowds,
Some distance from the day.

Sad world turns round, red sun goes down,
here is the end of another day.
Old spell is cast, cold night falls fast,
Seagulls wing out across the bay.

I am all, I am so small,
I often lose my way,
Among dark clouds, or tortured crowds,
Some distance from the day.

Striptease Joint

You can make up your own mind about whether this sentiment is true or imagined.

Written circa 1971

I visited a striptease joint,
but really failed to get the point!
In fact, I was disappointed -
I only got a stiff neck.

Weekend Treat

Around this time in my life I can remember that I had given up smoking ordinary cigarettes, and for maybe a few months only smoked a bit of wacky baccy at the weekends.

Written circa 1971

Sunday joint, followed by high tea.

Hand of God

Perhaps the wacky baccy made me think about spiritual matters. Who knows why things come into your head when your brain is addled by mild illegal stimulants.

Written circa 1971

Whilst stranded in the land of Nod
I landed in the hand of God;
his fingers were blue, and they were thin;
the angels said a prayer for me,
and offered me their sympathy,
and then they sang a hymn.

All this time
I've been trying to square the circle,
but the ends will never meet.
Make your sign;
You've been dying to turn the tables,
so the game will be complete.

No sooner was that said and done
when with the falling rain did come
dark promises of deep impending doom.
With blackness blocking out the sun,
upon a spider's web we hung,
and prayed for days for light to pierce the gloom.

Be yourself!
Never hide away your feelings!
Live and love in harmony!
Sing your song!
Keep in touch with your emotions!
Let your music set you free!

Sing your song!
Sing it loud, sing it long!
Let your music set you free!

CHAPTER 8

Now is the Time to Ramble on,
"On a spider's web suspended,
A beginning and the end,
In a clockwork constitution,
Status symbol minds pretend."

Backward Blues

This is 12 bar blues format with pretty stupid lyrics. Not very poetical, and not one of my best, or maybe it's weirdness is just the ticket? This period of my life wasn't very inspirational or productive, or maybe I was on a different planet?

Written circa 1972

As I got up one morning to see the sun go down;
As I got up one morning to see the sun go down;
I walked through the crowded city;
there was no one else around.

I jumped on to a bus, fifteen carriages long;
I jumped on to a bus, fifteen carriages long;
But when I looked around me
the captain he had gone.

I flew up to the Underground with my breakfast in my eyes;
I flew up to the Underground with my breakfast in my eyes;
Instead of staying on the ground
I walked up in the skies.

I handed my ticket to the dustman as he put the letters through the doors;
I handed my ticket to the dustman as he put the letters through the doors;
Just then I arrived in London;
on the Atlantic shores.

The birds were barking on the ground, the dogs sang in the trees;
The birds were barking on the ground, the dogs sang in the trees;
Jack Frost sat on the pavement
polishing his knees.

The mini-skirted boys all smiled and stood powdering their noses;
The mini-skirted boys all smiled, and stood powdering their noses;
Instead of giving me my wages this week
they had the cheek to give me a bunch of roses.

Crazy Paving

Here I am, away with the fairies again, but this time I think the old brain cells are working a bit harder to come up with something worthwhile. Maybe it's a bit too cryptic, but it was eventually recorded on a demo album called "Delicate Balancing Act" in September 2003.

Written originally circa 1972

Psychedelic perfumed dove,
Mephistopheles in love,
Here's the hand that fits the glove,
Matchsticks in the sky above,
Now you can step on my crazy paving stone baby,
You know I'm not alone.

Schizophrenic Brother John,
Ban the grass and keep the Bomb,
Alienated vision song,
Splits the rock with King Kong,
Now you can step on my crazy paving stone baby,
You know I'm not alone.

Fills the gap fantastically,
Simple Simon, you and me;
Patience waits most anxiously,
for Mandarin orange, and china tea,
Now you can step on my crazy paving stone baby,
You know I'm not alone.

Pluto's asking for a fight -
Punches pulled by satellite,
Apparitions in the night,
Metamorphosis in sight,
Now you can step on my crazy paving stone baby,
You know I'm not alone.

Jungle drums, red monkey tail;
Love by loved hits the nail,
Arrives on approval through the mail,
Words of silence cannot fail,
Now you can step on my crazy paving stone baby,
You know I'm not alone.

Earth

Worrying about the world you live in is a pretty natural thing to do in your early twenties I suppose, and in the 70's I think we may have been gently persuaded that our little home was a place with finite resources. Since then we seem to ask the question, "Where are we going with this?" nearly every day. We'd seen our beautiful home planet photographed from our space, and it gave anybody with a conscience a true perspective of how delicate our survival could really be.

Written circa 1972

A thousand million light years and a day, away,
beyond the darkness and the Milky Way, there lay,
A pearl among a purple empty sky,
A place where we belong; our planet Earth,
A place where we belong; our planet Earth.

Becomes a swollen, swallowed, hollow shell, a cell,
A graveyard where once was a wishing well, a hell,
A place without a face or tears to cry,
A place for our swansong; our planet Earth,
A place for our swansong; our planet Earth.

Black, desolate and eerie empty sphere, is here,
Suspended in dark shadow's living fear, so near,
A wilderness that waits and wonders why,
A place that we have wronged; our planet Earth,
A place that we have wronged; our planet Earth.

A thousand million light years and a day, away,
Beyond the darkness and the Milky Way, once lay,
A pearl among a purple empty sky,
A place where we belong; our planet Earth,
A place where we belong; our planet Earth.

Empty

A more reflective period in my writing history was beginning to emerge, and I was attempting to write in a more descriptive and sensitive way. I think there's bit more emotion in my words now.

Written circa 1972

Another lonely day draws to its close
and shadows of the night come flooding in.
I stand upon this wild and rocky shore,
and reminiscence flows again.

I hear the pounding ocean's timeless roar,
I watch the seagulls wing into the rain,
I sense the silent closing of a door,
I know I'll never be with you again.

Clear, cool and white the face of the new moon
arrives upon its easel in the sky,
as the mighty artist starts to paint the night
upon the canvas day disguised.

I smell the burning incense of the brine,
I watch the crashing waves break from their chains,
I feel so empty now within my heart,
I know I'll never see you here again.

Our sacrifices all in vain
when all is lost and nothing's gained;
our hopes for the future didn't last.
Remote, we watched what we became,
and as our chances waxed and waned
the sands of time were running out too fast.

Free

Then again, I can always lapse back into a frivolous mode. This could make a nice simple easy song, but it was never recorded.

Written circa 1972

When I stood there at your door
you didn't want me anymore;
Now I'm free baby free.
You told me that you were sure;
Same old lies I heard before;
Now I'm free baby free.

Left this town on the first train;
Now I ain't comin' back again;
Now I'm free baby free.
Spent all night out in the rain;
you're the one who's gone insane;
Now I'm free baby free.

Many suns and many a moon,
but it couldn't come too soon;
Now I'm free baby free.
Left last Friday afternoon;
you'll be missing me quite soon;
Now I'm free baby free.

You didn't even tell me why,
but I'm glad we said goodbye;
Now I'm free baby free.
What a feelin', my oh my!
Now I'd like to see you cry;
'Cause I'm free baby free,

Guitar song

There may have been times in early 70's when I felt my guitar was not only my best, but my only true friend. My long term mate Barry had moved to South Wales, casual girlfriends came and went in quick succession, and I was on shift work, where the weird sleeping patterns were crippling my brain. I still lived at home with my mum, and spent a lot of waking hours in pubs. But, once again, the emotional content comes through in this song. In time, the words were altered slightly and the song was recorded as "Best Friend" on the demo album "Only Turning Over Stones" in September 2000.

Written circa 1972

Had a dog long ago, but she died and I cried,
But I know I'll never be lonely
with my guitar by my side,
But I know I'll never be lonely
with my guitar by my side.

A home without a dog is like a dog without a home,
but I've still got one friend when I'm on my own,
but I've still got one friend, when I'm all alone.

Had a friend once to lean on, but she flew away you see,
but I know I'll never be lonely
with my guitar to comfort me,
But I know I'll never be lonely
with my guitar to comfort me.

Home without you is not any home at all,
but I've still got one friend I can always call,
but I've still got one friend.

Time to ramble on

Probably another good example of the way my writing was starting to develop towards a more descriptive process. I can remember being pleased with the over all poem/song. But it wasn't ever recorded in this form. Some of the words and constructions were "stolen" later, and went into different songs.

Written circa 1972

Red rays of the sunset on the grey green waters of the sea,
As the dying embers of the day fall down into eternity,
Lost among the ocean's swell the day has dropped into obscurity.

Now is the time to ramble on, now is the time to ramble on,
The time is now my friend, and soon we should be gone,
Now is the time to ramble on.

Catacomb-like city streets, they're litter strewn and grey with age,
Silent, sleepless, in the starlight's stolen hours upon the stage,
No truth here within the doorways, prisoners of history in a cage.

Now is the time to ramble on, now is the time to ramble on,
The time is now my friend, and soon we should be gone,
Now is the time to ramble on.

On a spider's web suspended a beginning and the end,
In a clockwork constitution status symbol minds pretend,
Happiness is everlasting, so the prophet's twisted words defend.

Now is the time to ramble on, now is the time to ramble on,
The time is now my friend, and soon we should be gone,
Now is the time to ramble on.

Dreaming in the lakeside moonlight, laughing in the summer rain,
For their muddled sense of values travelling people feel no pain,
Freedom is the bread of life, drives the wanderlust within your brain.

Now is the time to ramble on, now is the time to ramble on,
The time is now my friend, and soon we should be gone,
Now is the time to ramble on.

What is your share?

I might just be talking to myself here? At 23 I was floating and directionless, and at times felt like everybody and everything in the whole world was just manipulating me for its own purposes. Again, with hindsight I think now that working night shifts had a lot to do with this feeling. Many years later I remodelled this poem into something I hope is a bit more poetic.

Written circa 1972

Though you have survived those who have contrived
to warp your mind at school,
And you've bravely fought the sort that taught
that gun law is the best rule;
Dispel your illusions and reach the conclusion
that they use confusion as a tool.
Though you've broken your shackles, you can't win any battles,
If they continue to call you a fool.

You've explored corridors of the lame and the poor,
and the avenues all lead you away,
from the warmth of the womb to the gloom of the tomb,
from birth to return to the clay;
Dispel your illusions and make the conclusion
that they put confusion your way.
Though you've broken your shackles, you've lost all your battles,
If they continue to use you for play.

They arrange frequent change, but you're not think it strange
when the system is blind to your state.
Though the world in the future may possibly suit you,
and deep down inside you can't wait,

but have no illusions; throw out your confusion,
or you'll draw your conclusions too late.
Though you're free from your shackles, you've lost all your battles,
If they continue to use you for bait.

The social explosion of moral erosion
is just a sad fact that you bear.
Your pursuit of freedom gets further from Eden,
as now you've become more aware,
that to gain satisfaction you have to take action;
Show concern, but exercise care,
To be sure that your cure lies nearer to your ideas
of what is your share?

By extracting the facts and avoiding the traps
the jigsaw pieces will snap into place.
To endless confusion there will be a solution,
but beware of the dangers you face;
And to get satisfaction you'll need to take action,
and find your own way in the maze;
to be sure that your cure will show you the door
to the future you wish to create.

Wind of change

This poem was definitely written on a cold Winter's day, but there is more than a glimmer of hope in it for better times around the corner. I probably messed around for a long time with trying to turn this into a song, and eventually in a slightly different form it turned up as a recording in May 2001 on the demo album "Never Enough" as "Winter Song".
Note that my "Wind of Change" was written 18 years before the Scorpions recorded their song of the same name.

Written circa 1972

The naked tree, a frosty carcass, stripped of all its leaves,
Perched among the barrenness, the blanket Winter weaves,
Gripped by the frozen glassy skies, choked with new spun snows,
Aching in the watery sunshine of the Winter's throes.

But its back will not bend when Winter's at an end,
and Spring will bring a change in the wind,
So strong to defend, and a heart that's on the mend,
When Spring rings out a change in the wind.

Desolation shrouds the hillsides brown and ravaged shell.
How long, how long, till Spring's sweet chorus, breaks the Arctic spell?
Deep, so deep the country sleeps upon the diamond Earth,
through the echoes of the Summer till the Spring's rebirth.

The atmosphere suspends for the Snow Queen's reign to end
when Spring will bring a change in the wind,
Warmer greetings Nature sends, and a fresh new robe to lend
when Spring rings out a change in the wind.

When Mother Earth awakes to find the emotions Winter gripped;
Preserved among the timeless archives the icy hand has slipped;
Now just a blurred reflection in the season's passing page,
when Springtime celebrates again escape from Winter's rage.

When the wind of change it comes and Winter's on the run,
Spring brings a new season on the wind,
As the wind of change it blows, so the seasons come and go,
And Spring brings a new reason with the wind.

Previously Misquoted

No comment required really

Written circa 1972

"The penis; mightier than the sword?"

CHAPTER 9

A home without a dog
is like a dog without a home.

"Sixteen summers passed,
And you came along at last,
Someone that I'd been waiting for so long,
And you put your hand in mine,
We drank that good life wine,
Just for a while, together we belonged."

There wasn't much writing going on in this period, because I am still probably trying to find my niche. I don't know what I'm good at, and what I'm crap at, and so I try lots of different ways to put things down in words without feeling much fulfilment. "Song to Annis" is probably my best bit of writing in this chapter, and it still comes through as a truly experienced emotional expression. Some of the other stuff is either "disposable" or depressing.

Song to Annis.

Long ago, when I was very young, I knew someone called Annis Harrison. She was very precious to me, but I knew it was only a matter of time before she would "want to travel on". This was probably the first song with any long term quality that I had ever written. These are the original words.

Written February 1973

Sixteen summers passed, and she came along at last;
Someone that I'd been waiting for so long.
She let me steal her time; she let me drink her wine,
She showed me where the Universe belonged.

Annis every morning I rise with your name upon my lips,
And I'll be thinking of you all day long,
Annis there's a bird that flies, the reddest of our sunset skies,
Winging homeward bringing you this song.

Daisy chains are spun, in the summer sun,
Though the seeds are sown in crisp white winter days,
The balance is so fine, our chance to fill the time,
With flowers gathered from our narrow ways.

Annis every morning I rise with your name upon my lips,
And I'll be thinking of you all day long,
Annis there's a bird that flies, the reddest of our sunset skies,
Winging homeward bringing you this song.

Oh how can I compare, your beautiful dark hair,
To any summer's day when you are gone,
You are so very young; your journey's just begun,
And one day you will want to travel on.

Annis every morning I rise with your name upon my lips,
And I'll be thinking of you all day long,
Annis there's a bird that flies, the reddest of our sunset skies,
Winging homeward bringing you this song.

By the time a version of the song was recorded at Amber Studios in November 2000 on the album "Beyond Pure Extremes" the words had been transformed as below.

Sixteen summers passed,
And you came along at last,
Someone that I'd been waiting for so long,
And you put your hand in mine;
We drank that good life wine,
Just for a while, together we belonged.
Annis every morning I rise with your name upon my lips
And I'll be thinking of you all day long.
Annis there's a bird that flies
the reddest of our sunset skies,
Winging homeward,
Bringing you this song.

Daisy chains were spun
in the summer sun;
Though the seeds were sown in crisp white winter days,
The balance was so fine,
Our chance to fill the time,
With flowers gathered from our narrow ways.
Annis every morning I rise with your name upon my lips
And I'll be thinking of you all day long.
Annis there's a bird that flies
the reddest of our sunset skies,
Winging homeward,
Bringing you this song.

You surely were aware,
The time drew ever nearer
For only lonely days when you'd be gone.
You were so very young,
Your journey had just begun
And one day soon you'd want to travel on.
Annis every morning I rise with your name upon my lips
And I'll be thinking of you all day long.
Annis there's a bird that flies
the reddest of our sunset skies,
Winging homeward,
Bringing you this song.

Best friend

This poem/song started off a few years before as "Guitar Song" and then finally emerged as "Best Friend" on a demo called "Only Turning Over Stones" recorded at Amber Studios in September 2000.

Written circa 1975

Had a dog long ago, but she died and I cried,
But I know I'll never be lonely
with my best friend by my side,
But I know I'll never be lonely
with my best friend by my side.

A home without a dog is like a dog without a home,
But I've still got one friend when I'm on my own,
But I've still got one friend when I'm all alone.

Had a friend once to lean on, but she flew away you see,
But I know I'll never be lonely
with my best friend to comfort me,
But I know I'll never be lonely
with my best friend to comfort me.

Home without you is not any home at all,
But I've still got one friend I can always call.
But I've still got one friend.

Campfire/Cowboy song

I stole the idea for this from a Jasper Carrot style folksinger/ guitarist/ raconteur/ comedian called Stan Arnold. Sorry Stan!
Some of the words/constructions are mine and some (like the chorus) are a direct lift, but I couldn't remember all the original lyrics, and so I had to make up my own. If I remember correctly, Stan introduces it at a song that he and Jim Reeves wrote together while on a long cow trail from Wyoming to Texas. Although I've sung this song many times it was never recorded.

Written circa 1975

NOTE: Requires frequent ad-libs of: "Aw Shucks!" and "Yee Haa!"

I was sitting by the campfire picking my nose,
Using my toothbrush to clean between my toes,
And I've had nothing but baked beans for my tea.
Out here on the prairie the piles are giving me hell,
I've ate so many beans that I'm jet propelled,
And I don't know who smells worse my old horse or me.

Yippee yi yo,
Yippee yi ye,
I love to see them udders sway,
I want to be a cowpoke,
Just poking cows all day.

Well sometimes I might get drunk,
I Walk like a duck and I smell like a skunk,
I need another shot of redeye to keep me hairy.
I've got a girl in Medicine Bow,
She's got thighs like tugboats and a face like a sow;
She makes Clint Eastwood look more like Julian Clary.

Yippee yi yo,
Yippee yi ye,
I love to see them udders sway,
I want to be a cowpoke,
Just poking cows all day.

I ain't going to hit this trail no more,
My heart is heavy and my arse is sore,
And it looks like it's coming on to rain.
I know a girl called Calamity Jane,
She only likes it now and again,
And again and again and again and again and again.

Yippee yi yo,
Yippee yi ye,
I love to see them udders sway,
I want to be a cowpoke,
Just poking cows all day.

Sitting by the campfire picking my teeth,
Using my toothbrush to scrape me underneath,
I've got skid marks up to my shoulder blades.
Sitting by the campfire lighting my farts,
Being careful not to singe my private parts,
I'm the secret weapon on those renegade Indian raids.

Yippee yi yo,
Yippee yi ye,
I love to see them udders sway,
I want to be a cowpoke,
Just poking cows all day.

Well a cowboy's life is really rough;
You gotta be strong and you gotta be tough,
And you gotta do it all with great sincerity.
I hear the sound of distant drums,
(That's the bit Jim Reeves wrote. Same old rubbish!)
And Country and Western guitar strums,
And a record contract for my mate Jim and me.

Yippee yi yo,
Yippee yi ye,
I love to see them udders sway,
I want to be a cowpoke,
Just poking cows all day.

Cry out for you

I'm going into the depths of despair by the looks of it. Far too far down a bottomless pit to be anything but a miserable poem, but some of the words were later stolen for other songs/poems

Written circa 1975

In the clouds of such confusion
I stare at the shadowed sign
that directs me to seclusion;
leaving troubles far behind,
I see faces in the mirror;
I know none of them is mine,
I am losing fast my senses;
My defences undermined.

I cry out for you,
I cry out for you,
I cry out for you.

While stabbing pains of jealousy
throw red before my eyes;
No cooling calm of whisper winds
to soothe or hypnotise;
No healing hands in soft caress;
No cosy compromise,
I'm searching out insanity,
But it's heavily disguised.

I cry out for you,
I cry out for you,
I cry out for you.

Original title was "Opus 16983"
But was eventually re-titled "Destiny"

This is more than likely just an extension of the previous gloomy sentiment, but I hope it's a bit better poetically. I don't know why it was called "Opus 16983" because it's hardly a major piece of work. By the time it becomes transformed into a never recorded song called "Destiny" I feel much better about its value as a poem/song.

Written circa 1975

Now once again I stand alone
upon the tightrope line,
Along which trod no men of God
to leave a guiding sign,
Through centuries of history,
Held by some evil spell,
I balanced there, and wondered where,
The heroes had all fell,
The heroes had all fell.

The sun rose up in eastern mists
across the plains of time;
Left me marooned, alone and doomed,
A prisoner for no crime.
Then, all at once, headlong I fell,
Upon which side; heaven or hell?
Until I land, my soul is damned,
And I am falling still,
And I am falling still.

Passing time

After a short period of morose scribbling I come back to reality and a more everyday life kind of feel. This was written as song, and was sung a few times, but never recorded.

Written circa 1975

I lead the life of a very simple man,
And the open road is my home.
The trees and the flowers and the birds are my friends,
And my home is where my soul wants to roam.
How does this compare with you my friend;
It you sit down and think about it?
When you lead your humdrum workaday life,
Well, I can just do without it.

Well your life may be very fine for you,
And you think that it's alright,
When you sit on your high horse in the local bar,
And get drunk on a Saturday night,
Go to Church on a Sunday, go to work on Monday,
And Tuesday's just another day,
Get bored on a Wednesday,
Get depressed on the Thursday,
And Friday's yet another wasted day.

Whereas I am as free as the summer breeze,
And my home is where my soul wants to roam,
I will stay here a while, and sleep under the trees,
And when I get on my feet I move on.
How does this compare with you my friend;
If you sit down and think about it?
When you lead your humdrum workaday life,
Well I can just do without it.

Time is passing you by;
Ever faster it flies!
Life in the backroom is no longer thrilling.
Time is the vacuum you should be filling.
Time is not something you should be killing,
Until you are willing to die,
Until you're willing to die.

CHAPTER 10

And the Walls came Tumbling Down

"There is a time that we call now,
The pace has quickened up somehow,
Our Earth is used,
Time in suspense,
The season of our affluence."

Here are some more extracts from the unpublished book "Taking Chances, Making Choices". This time they cover the period from 1980 to 1989.

Taking Chances, Making Choices

CHAPTER 10

The Old Order Crumbles

A six year long tradition had evolved, where all the boys would congregate at Brian's house on Cup Final Day to watch the game and have (more than) a few beers. In 1980 there was an extra edge. Brian had been an Arsenal supporter since he had been a child. I don't know where that came from; him being a Cockney and a (mostly) Essex boy, but nevertheless since this year the final was to be between West Ham and Arsenal we were definitely set for a brilliant afternoon. By 5 p.m., I knew just how brilliant! The Hammers had beaten the Gunners 1-0. Brian was "Bloody annoyed", but I couldn't help but chuckle at our victory, especially since my heroes were in the 2nd division at the time...

In 1981 Rosemary fell pregnant again, proving the previously feared adage about "New Home, New Baby"; but at least she had waited a decent interval this time as we had been in our new home over a year. Sadly, early on in the pregnancy she came into accidental contact, in the doctor's surgery of all places, with some children suffering from German measles, and after much heart searching she agreed that it was best to have the pregnancy terminated...

In the early 80's for 3 years, we had been having traditional seaside holidays every year in Aberystwyth. After a disastrous rain filled in 2 weeks in September 1982, Rosemary was determined to persuade me to go abroad to sunnier climes. After our first "foreign" holiday in May 1983 in Lloret de Mar on the Costa Brava, we never looked back, regularly going to Spain every year for 9 years. In 1985 we switched to the Costa Blanca, staying in the Hotel Tropicana in Benidorm. My dad and his new partner Joan had at that time recently sold up in England, and moved to their dream home; a villa in the Jalon valley, just a few miles inland from Denia, and about 20 miles from Benidorm through the mountains of the Col de Rates.

We had a superb holiday; the weather was blistering, spending a few days additionally at Dad's villa. There was a strange eerie feeling to the "hasta la vista" at our hotel on the last night of our holiday, as I shook my dad's hand, I felt impelled to give him a big hug, and he seemed somehow at peace, more contented than I had seen him for a long time, in his "paradise found"...

Over the moon

In 1985 City of Westminster took a dramatic and irreversible swerve in a different direction. Echoing central government the council appointed a woman, Lady Shirley Porter as leader. It wasn't difficult to imagine Shirley popping up the road and having working lunches on a regular basis with her friend Margaret. They heralded the era of assertive and sometimes frightening women in power. Lady Porter's initial technology project involved changing the status of the council to one that she considered appropriate for Westminster's prominence as a well-behaved Tory administration toeing the central government line.

With a certainty unshakeable, she insisted that we ditch our Sperry Univac mainframe in favour of becoming a mainstream IBM user. In a few short months we became an IBM site, and I was interviewed and appointed as Computer Support Manager, responsible for every aspect of support; Operations, Production, Systems, Minicomputers, Personal Computing, and Telecommunications. Overnight I'd joined the Yuppie club!

Suddenly there was a generous salary outside local government pay structures, and a company car, and best of all the freedom to develop and innovate in the Information Technology field to the ultimate benefit of the council. The quill pens had been scratching for far too long behind their heavy wooden desks. Here was an opportunity to be part of the biggest I.T. revolution seen in local government anywhere, and echoing the "Big Bang" revolution taking place in financial institutions in the City of London...

Under a cloud

We had been on holiday in Majorca in August 1987 and liked it so much that we had re-booked to coincide with my sister Sylvia's family holiday there in October. Together with my mother we set of for Gatwick in the small hours of the morning, only to find that an unprecedented thunderstorm had knocked out Air Traffic Control for the Western Mediterranean. A 16 hour wait at Gatwick was endured before we arrived in El Arenal almost a day later than scheduled.

As if this wasn't sufficient aggravation, following this second visit of the year to Majorca we arrived back in England only 4 days before the famous hurricane struck the South East with such immense devastation. My sister Sylvia and her family were not so lucky; returning from the same holiday destination on the night the hurricane hit, and within feet of landing at Gatwick before an emergency aborted landing and subsequent diversion to East Midlands airport...

When Black Monday came on 19th October 1987 and the Stock Market crashed, it was already evident that the Thatcher bubble was fit for bursting, and her unfortunate demise beckoned on the horizon.

The Main Chance

Back at work the major opportunity of my career was about to present itself. By 1987 the combination of our switch to IBM, and the explosive demand for technology on the desk in the form of networked personal computing, set the stage for my finest hour...

Hammers and horrors

My few appearances at Upton Park as a real supporter had dwindled away to almost nothing, but after many mediocre years in the First Division, and a run of lack lustre results that had then glued to the bottom spot, West Ham were relegated to Division 2 again at the end of the 88/89 season. Saddened though I was, this minor annoyance paled into insignificance against something that had happened a few weeks before. The date 15th April will always be remembered by every kind of football supporter, perhaps throughout the world.

What should have been a celebration of all that is good about English football, and especially the FA Cup, turned into the saddest indictment of what was becoming an anonymous and remote big money business rather than a spectator sport belonging to real people. The spectators of the match between Liverpool and Nottingham Forest came with glad expectation to see an exhibition match at Hillsborough...

Times they are a changin'

My talent for presenting to all levels of the council - staff, directors and members, (councillors), found me, during 1989, making regular presentations to committee meetings on technology matters. In addition I was able to enjoy illustrating Westminster's network projects to a stream of interested contemporaries in the telecommunications and computing fields.

Career-wise the period between 1985 and 1990 was my most successful and personally fulfilled time. My most successful group of years was echoed by world events, culminating in a tumultuous change of the old communist/capitalist confrontation in 1989...

Gorbachev gambles

Solidarity gained victory in the Polish elections after the ban on their organisation had been lifted in April, and by August, Mazowiecki became the first non-Communist leader in the Iron Bloc.

On 11th September Hungary opened its borders to the west, and then throughout the soviet satellite states crude eastern bloc vehicles, like the laughably antiquated Trabbies, converged on Hungary and invaded capitalist Europe. Citizens across the planet waited for what had historically so far been a predictable and expected Russian "Iron fist" reaction. A visionary Mikael Gorbachev failed to be dragged into the predictable and previously well rehearsed "friendly" invasion.

Could these run down, oppressed states dare to defy the Russian bear?...

CHAPTER 11

Delusions of Grandeur

"If only I was young again,
With yearning heart and burning then,
For words to rise and quickly grow,
From pen to paper, ebb and flow,
Can substitute there ever be,
For youthful creativity?"

Bugger the neighbours.

I wrote this song while I was on a week-long computer programming course in Birmingham. It was probably the words of a sage like Alf Garnett who provided the inspiration. It's a bit of tongue in cheek, because you've got to love your bloody neighbours. Recorded at Amber Studios in November 2000 on the demo album called "Beyond Pure Extremes".

Written February 1980

When you're having a party on a Saturday night,
and you turn up the music and turn down the lights,
and a wild raging bull comes to bang on your door;
It's that humourless boring old fart from next door.
Just say bugger the neighbours
and their greener grass;
Bugger the neighbours;
they can all kiss my arse.
Just say bugger the neighbours,
And before they're much older;
May their ear holes become arseholes
and shit on their shoulders.

When you've had a bad day and you're getting the strop,
and you come home to barney and argue non-stop,
and you raise up your voice and let it all out,
If you live down my street you will hear me shout.
I'll say bugger the neighbours
and their greener grass;
Bugger the neighbours;
they can all kiss my arse.
I'll say bugger the neighbours,
And before they're much older;
May their ear holes become arseholes

and shit on their shoulders.

When you're sat on the bog; had a curry last night,
and you squit and you strain till your knuckles go white,
and you let rip a fart like a plane coming in,
They can hear you next door 'cause the walls are so thin.
Just say bugger the neighbours
and their greener grass;
Bugger the neighbours;
they can all kiss my arse.
Just say bugger the neighbours,
And before they're much older;
May their ear holes become arseholes
and shit on their shoulders.

When you're up for some shagging; all tense and uptight,
and you're sure in your trousers tonight is the night;
then you get horizontal and give it your all,
And the headboard goes bang, bang, bang, bang on the wall;
Just say bugger the neighbours
and their greener grass;
Bugger the neighbours;
they can all kiss my arse.
Just say bugger the neighbours,
And before they're much older;
May their ear holes become arseholes
and shit on their shoulders.

So maybe it's hard for your dreams to come true
when the bastards next door are much richer than you;
So just smile and walk by as they turn up their noses,
and send the dog out at night to shit on their roses.
Just say bugger the neighbours
and their greener grass;
Bugger the neighbours;
they can all kiss my arse.
Just say bugger the neighbours,
And before they're much older;
May their ear holes become arseholes
and shit on their shoulders.

Delusions of Grandeur

I don't know who this is about, but it's not a cheap imitation of "where do you go to my Lovely" by Peter Starstedt. It is far more acidic and much less whimsical.

Written circa 1980

You think you're a gold ballerina,
admired in your little glass case,
and you feel that no one can touch you,
and only a few selected few can see your face.
You know there's nothing between us,
except forgotten words which passed long ago;
Your nonchalance is all that can screen you
from realising that you move too slow.

And I get to thinking sometimes
if you're really conscious of the way your going.
I wonder if you remember anything they taught you
in all of those high class schools;
When every move you make is controversial,
and often leaves inadequacies showing;
Though inhibitions cast aside
and every effort's made to hide
yet another breach of the rules.

Now you're clandestine love affair
with an eccentric millionaire
terminated on the first of June;
When he proposed to you, you froze,
and in a frantic rage you chose
to close the honeymoon;
And you think that ecstasy
 is sex to me, and you,
and millions more
upon this speck of dust that we call Earth.
You strove for popularity,
and forgot your singularity;
a burden you have shouldered since your birth.

If I could turn the clock back a year or two;
a second time I'd emerge from the mist,
But time has erased all trace of the evidence
to prove that I ever did exist;
And now I hear that in the very next week
you'll have your own stand at an exhibition;
You'll be ignored
and feel you're a freak,
and everyone will be bored with your repetition.

And when it seems that all that's left is shattered dreams,
and the nightmare of reality is knocking on your door;
Well you and me, fait accompli, it's over, finished, done,
and for all that can be said let's say no more.
I'm all for letting sleeping dogs lie, and let the time go by,
forget the past and look for things to come;
Another breach of sacred rules made for fools,
but you'll keep learning by the rule of thumb.

Loss of inspiration

If I wrote this round about 1980, then I was 31 and starting to worry about my future in a very different way. By then I was married, with a daughter, 4 years old, and I was starting at last to make real inroads into a proper career in computers and telecomms, while living in a brand house with a hefty mortgage. A lot of things had changed in 5 or 6 years since I had been a footloose, part-time hippy, living at home with my mum.

Written circa 1980

The dagger of reality
has thrust its rusted blade in me;
No purple dreams, no fantasies,
to bring forth creativity;
The clock has ticked, long ages spent,
So seldom inspiration sent.

To steal the poet's zeal again,
Let magic gems flow from the pen,
And tear the dusty sheets apart,
With stirring words straight from the heart.

So sad the passing bloom of youth
that holds reality aloof;
And as we grow long in the tooth,
Sad eyes reveal distorted truth;
Experience the saving grace
to take enthusiasm's place.

If only I was young again,
With yearning heart and burning then,
For words to rise and quickly grow,
From pen to paper, ebb and flow;
Can substitute there ever be,
For youthful creativity?

Male Chauvinist Pig Blues

This is a throwaway rant, written on a relentless surge of women's liberation, and is not to be taken at all seriously.

Written circa 1980

I'm an MCP,
so don't bug me
with your silly ideas of women's liberty.

I'm An MCP;
You don't dig me,
'Cause female emancipation doesn't get my sympathy.

I'm an MCP,
and you can't tell me
that a man and a woman can reverse polarity.

I'm an MCP,
so don't bother me
with your high-flown hopes of sex equality.

I'm an MCP,
and all I want to see
is a little femininity.

Who cares anyway?

Oh my God, here I am, down in the dumps again with a common, recurring theme. Somebody has pissed on my chips, and I'm going into a rant about it again for probably no good reason.

Written circa 1980

And I told you time and time again;
You never heeded my warning.
You listened but you did not hear,
You looked but you did not see,
You sensed but you could not feel,
You should have taken far more notice of me,
You just shrugged your shoulders and said,
Who cares anyway?
Who cares anyway?
Who cares anyway?
Who cares anyway?

And I tell you time and time again;
You never heed my warning.
You listen but you do not hear,
You look but you do not see,
You sense but you can not feel,
You should take far more notice of me,
You just shrug your shoulders and say,
Who cares anyway?
Who cares anyway?
Who cares anyway?
Who cares anyway?

And I will tell you time and time again;
You will never heed my warning.
You will listen but you will not hear,
You will look but you will not see,
You will sense but you're unable to feel,
You should be taking far more notice of me,
And not just shrug your shoulders and say,
Who cares anyway?
Who cares anyway?
Who cares anyway?
Who cares anyway?

Writing on the wall

It's the1980's and the media has started to bombard us all with information about the cataclysmic events that will befall our unbeloved planet if we carry on with our relentless exploitation of its resources. So I had to write something about it to warn everybody.

Written circa 1980

There was a time we called the past;
The pace of life was not too fast,
Our Earth was fresh,
Our time was spring,
The season of our wandering.
With innocence around us all
there was no writing on the wall.
Wise prophets deemed there was no call
to carve the writing on the wall.

There is a time that we call now;
The pace has quickened up somehow,
Our Earth is used,
Time in suspense,
The season of our affluence.
Our knowledge of the present calls
to read the writing on the wall;
It screams in headlines ten feet tall;
Now, heed the writing on the wall.

There'll be a time that we call then;
The pace will quicken once again,
Our Earth all spent,
Our time long gone,
The season of our dying swan.
The past and present tell us all,
To read the writing on the wall,
It won't be long till we recall,
When there was writing on the wall.

Miracle

Now this is more like it! I don't know what the inspiration was, but I've always been highly delighted with this bit of work. It tends to portray a bit of deeper thinking, with more obscurity in the words, but a strong theme of an irresistible force moving towards an immovable mass. But I always felt it was never finished. So, in an amended form, with an extra verse, it will turn up again later on as a poem/song called "Elegy"

Written originally in 1980,

A dazzling nightmare focussed on a crocus head of fire;
Burns the blackened fingers of the saint upon his pyre,
And reaches out to grasp the hands that stretches taut the wire,
Balancing the quaint and painted faces of the choir.

Through the mystic harmonies the melancholy song;
A magic, tragic symphony of theories right and wrong,
Is played through frayed and tattered winds on sailing ships of old,
That roll and pitch the cursed witch who turns the world to gold.

And now an orange cloud is swirling high above our heads;
It needs to find a resting place among the living dead,
Between the far-flung provinces where broken prophets kneel,
To curse the Earth that scorned their birth and stopped their spinning wheel.

Now Heaven lies between the milestones of this Roman road;
Each step you take towards the gate of iron spottiswode,
Is fixed betwixt the sailing ships whose rotting hulks of rust,
Still roll and pitch the cursed witch who turns the world to dust.

Boob gazing

My little family unit spent a lot of holiday time on the Costas in the 80's, and this poem/song (never recorded) was a bit of tongue in cheek bravado written in the lazy sunshine days, heavily sedated by Champan and San Miguel, and an excessive amount of all-inclusive buffet meals.

Written in Benidorm, circa 1985

When you've had your fill of San Miguel,
And you've done the trip to Guadalest,
And you've swallowed your pride on the donkey ride,
And got pissed on the Lemon Express,
Your pesetas start to peter out
'cause you've been round all of the shops,
Then its time to go down to the beach boys,
And join in with top of the flops.

You can go boob gazing, it's amazing,
Boob gazing, when the sun is blazing,
Knocker watching, double scotching,
Topless bathing, nothing retaining 'em,
It ain't no crime to spend your time
prospecting for titanium.

Some people I know decided to go
to Benidorm on their holidays,
And they sat in the sun from just after one,
Till the sun went down on the bay.
Now, she was quite flat, had nothing of that,
And she started to peel like a prawn;
He said "Gord Blimey mate if she peels at that rate,
Then the little she's got will be gone."

You can go boob gazing, it's amazing,
Boob gazing, when the sun is blazing,
Knocker watching, double scotching,
Topless bathing, nothing retaining 'em,
It ain't no crime to spend your time
prospecting for titanium.

Now if you're obsessed with the sight of the breast,
When you're laying down by the foam,
Then the best place to go, as every man knows,
Is where the topless ladies do roam,
With the other half sitting there,
it's not something you share,
And she may come on to moan,
So just tell her it's alright where you get your appetite,
Just as long as you eat at home.
You can go boob gazing, it's amazing,
Boob gazing, when the sun is blazing,
Knocker watching, double scotching,
Topless bathing, nothing retaining 'em,
 It ain't no crime to spend your time
prospecting for titanium.

When it time to go there's a question to pose,
So I'll leave you now with a quiz,
The answer I've pondered for longer and longer,
And I still don't know what it is,
Us men have our game, and we're all the same,
You girls will agree to that,
But while we're boob gazing, the question it's raising,
Is, what the are you girls staring at?

It must be, crotch watching, sausage boxing,
Thong wearing, size comparing,
Lunch box glaring, todger staring,
Rumpo dreaming, knicker creaming;
It's such a surprise if you say to the guys
that size doesn't matter at all.

CHAPTER 12

Hurricanes and other Disasters

"Our Earth is used,
Time in suspense,
The season of our affluence,
Our knowledge of the present calls,
To read the writing on the wall,
It screams in headlines ten feet tall,
Now, heed the writing on the wall."

Here's another extract from the unpublished book "Taking Chances, Making Choices". This time it covers the period from 1990 to 1995.

Taking Chances, Making Choices

CHAPTER 12

1990 to 1995 Changes

In 1990 my work situation changed. Till then, I had a very fulfilling and rewarding career in computing and telecommunications. At that time I was working for the City of Westminster Council, and as was the fashion they decided that the accountants would take over the world.

What this meant was that the computer and telecommunications operations would be privatised, and as usual the refugees from this exercise would be the personnel who "occupied" the various management positions. In 1991 they employed a character called Peter Woodward, known by many as "Wiggy", to be responsible for overseeing this privatisation project. He illustrated numerous talents related to people, management, Information Technology, and especially good manners.

A new combination of stresses were generated. The excesses of a lifestyle with a substantial salary, company car, and other benefits, combined to see me drinking far too much as a crutch for the forthcoming Armageddon. That was, the awful day when I would be made redundant...

Celebration

To give an example of the height of my inability to cope with the stress, and to emphasise the trapdoor that I persisted in falling through repeatedly to ease the pain with alcohol, I illustrate this incident.

In November 1992, we were invited to a christening party at my niece Karen's house for her son Daniel. This took place on a Sunday afternoon, and the party began at about 4 p.m. It began quietly like any other party, and I had no inkling of what was to come. It seems that very quickly I drank nearly half a bottle of Southern Comfort, something I don't even like, and became totally inebriated, on the point of collapse. We had to return home, and Michelle's boyfriend Kevin drove us in my company car back to our house some 20 miles away. I was practically unconscious, and knew nothing of what was going on.

I can recollect waking up in my own bed at about 5 o'clock the next morning and feeling like my head was being hammered with a pneumatic drill.

Everybody in the family understood. They all thought "Poor old Mick, he's going to be made redundant in a few weeks time, it really no surprise that he should lose control."

Another example of me coping by blocking out reality with alcohol...

Turning my hand

As if to demonstrate my wide-ranging versatility I began to apply for manual jobs, and to play down all my previous experience. It worked!

At my next interview I was offered a job on the night shift at B & Q as a shelf-stacker. It was of no consequence that my earnings had plummeted from over £23.00 to £3.25 an hour.

Within 4 months I was supervisor, narrowly failing to acquire the recently vacated Shift Manager's position due to my lack of retail experience.

There was no question who ran the shift and who sat on his laurels in the office, and no doubt who the people's choice was. The work was hard, physical, and back in the dead mind and body syndrome of night shifts, but I was popular with all the other workers, and enjoyed what I was doing...

When I became a Driving Instructor, everyone said that it was a very stressful job. The process of teaching, and especially teaching people how to drive, can be inherently stressful, but a lot depends on how you go about it.

Once established, I found the most stressful aspect of this employment was worrying about whether there would be enough work to make the job worth-while, and pay the bills. Adverts suggested a £16,000 per annum salary achievable, but £6,000 was nearer the truth. The driver instruction industry was viciously competitive, lesson fees falling, and running expenses ever rising...

Keeping it in the family

Rosemary and myself were married in 1974. It had at times been a stormy marriage, with its fair collection of ups and downs, but she had always stuck by me, and through thick and thin we had stayed together. The early 90's was a difficult period for both of us, Rosemary had work and health problems of her own, and our Michelle had become that awful raging monster called a teenager. In the early 90's, with the imminent redundancy hanging over me, until on 31st December 1992 it actually happened, and then the over £40,000 a year salary was gone, the company car had gone, and the self-respect had gone. As a family we had a very stormy and turbulent few years.

In January 1996 Rosemary and I began to attend Relate sessions to try and get better communication and understanding between us. There was no magic wand, and what happened was that we discussed and sorted out our problems guided by the counsellor...

Couch potato?

In my early teens, I did take the opportunity to watch football matches with my Dad, or with friends of my own age. My Dad supported Romford Town Football Club, and we were frequent spectators to their home matches at Brooklands before the local property developers condemned the club to death when they bought the land occupied by the football ground. This scenario was sadly repeated at Brentwood Town and Chelmsford City some years later.

I also attended some professional football matches in East London, going to Brisbane Road to support Leyton Orient during their brief "glory years".

I supported the 'O's throughout the most successful period in their history, when in the 1962/63 season they were runners up in the old Second Division to Liverpool, and won promotion to the First Division. Whereas Liverpool went on to ever greater and greater accolades, poor old unfortunate Orient were out-classed, and were relegated back to Division Two in their first season in the top flight. I also went to football matches at the Boleyn Ground, now known as

Upton Park, and supported West Ham United through their triumph in the F. A. Cup Final in 1963/64. It was a rare privilege to see the core of the Hammers team, Hurst, Moore, and Peters, instrumental in taking the World Cup for England in 1966.

Michael was a good sport!

As a child I had always been rather skinny and spindly. As a teenager I had developed quickly and grown substantially in height over a short period, this made me extremely self-conscious of my thin-ness in my teenage years, and I therefore shied away from taking part in any event that involved spectators. When I was at Shenfield Technical School as a 6th former, we were permitted to use the school swimming pool unsupervised at lunchtime. I took advantage of this two or three times a week. Because I was with my classmates only, who had got used to my lack of physical frame, having seen me in the gymnasium, I was less self-consciousness during these unsupervised swimming sessions...

An even more abject lesson in the revered status of repeatedly coming last was learned in the process of entering, or to be more precise being entered for every event on school sports day.

A few seconds after finishing last in the 100 yards sprint, I found myself obliged to dash over to the putting the shot competition, and after taking the loser's place again, had to hurry back to come last again in the 220 yards running event. I considered myself lucky not to have to run all 4 legs of the 4 x 400 yards relay...

Oh Yes, I'm the Great Pretender

From age 37 onwards, and for seven years running, I participated in a single sporting occasion; the Sunday Times Fun Run in Hyde Park. I entered into my age heat every year except 1991, when I took part in the Mass Jog due to a recurrent back problem. On the last weekend of September each year this became a regular family event with almost everyone in the immediate family participating in not only the picnic in Hyde Park but also the running.

The course consisted of a temporary grass track covering 2.5 miles, (4 Kms), going to every corner of the park, in and around the groups of mature trees, circling the nursery, and finishing down by the Serpentine after snaking along, up, and down every possible incline.

My results, which I am proud of nevertheless, were as follows: -

Date	Position out of Category		Time
28th September, 1986	991 of ????	Men 36/38	not recorded
27th September, 1987	937 of 993	Men 36/38	22.40
25th September, 1988	1198 of 1290	Men 39/42	23.30
24th September, 1989	1087 of 1138	Men 39/42	23.50
30th September, 1990	730 of 841	Men 39/42	21.50
6th October, 1991	N/A	Mass Jog	26.00
27th September, 1992	546 of 600	Men 43/49	23.20

In order to be able to tackle this event, it was necessary to go into some form of training. I trained with due seriousness and dedication for three months before each event, beginning with only short distances of possibly 100 to 200 yards, and then building up gradually until by the time the day came I had covered at least two miles on a number of occasions. Besides ensuring that this limited my consumption of alcohol and food, there were other benefits. It was during one of these training periods that I at last successfully gave up smoking on a long-term basis. Another beneficial aspect was that I resisted the temptation to go to the pub with the boys at work at lunchtime, and instead went on long walks in and around the various tourist attractions in the City of Westminster. The benefit of not drinking 2 or 3 pints at lunchtime may have been outweighed by the pollution from the traffic fumes?

Perhaps the Sunday Times Fun Runs were a throwback to my cross-country running days at school? I remember the euphoria of coming round the last bend in the circuit, and having the home straight in sight, cheered on by the spectators. For a few moments I felt like a celebrity, and revelled in the sense of achievement in finishing the course. I usually came in the 900 to 1000 places in this very well supported bracket, finishing in about 22 minutes, but it did not matter. This genuinely was the pleasure of taking part, winning was never a possibility...

Aggressors and accountants

It wasn't long before the new order, with just the United States left to the onerous duty of acting as policemen for the world's stability, was forced to flex its collective muscle after the Iraqi despot; Saddam Hussein occupied Kuwait in early August of 1990. Diplomacy played out, as another dictator's miscalculation resulted in failure, when with the joint task forces that became Operation Desert Storm initiated the ground war on 23rd February. Kuwait City was recaptured in 3 days, and Saddam agreed to a cease-fire on 28th February 1991.

Blown away

Further re-orders of the world's political and national structures followed with the dissolution of the Warsaw pact in 1991, and the break up of the Russian dominated Soviet empire into smaller, easier to manage, but inherently more nationalistic sovereign states.

The new super power at Westminster council, a certain Mr W. Roots had been appointed City Treasurer, and promised to wreak an accountant's backlash on the too expensive and too powerful smart arse yuppies of the IT group. He appointed a devious assistant to carry out the cathartic process. This single-minded person, affectionately known as "Wiggy" by his intended victims, was also secretly labelled Supreme Head of Information Technology, (S.H.I.T.). Wiggy was a man who was more than adequately equipped to sell his soul to the devil for a few gold coins, who denied that any of his fellow men had any value or integrity.

By mid 1992 the end was drawing near. The bubble had already burst when Shirley Porter had been discredited over the "Homes for Votes" scandal and a new altogether more ruthless and significantly less sensitive regime was about to bare it's brown teeth, and bite where it hurt most.

Mr. Woodward took an instant dislike to me, but through all his taunts and ill judged insults I never once rose to his tainted bait...

Whimpering and wallowing

As I left my office for the final time on the evening of 30th December 1992, going out with a whimper rather than a bang, mostly due to the normal post-Xmas lull, the full impact of my situation had not truly hit home. Soon after New Year, Rosemary and myself took refuge in our first winter holiday, staying at the Hotel Honolulu in Palma Nova in Majorca for one week...

We returned on 18th January, and on 20th January I was obliged to return my Cavalier SRI, my company car, to the council. Unknown to me until arrival at Westminster, everyone else who had been made redundant also returned their cars that day, and a very boozy and boisterous reunion afternoon was held in the Greencoat Boy and Vincent's Wine Bar downstairs...

On 20th February we held an enormous mock retirement party at home, well attended by all our friends, relatives and neighbours, all of who could not believe how well I was adjusting to my new situation...

Pipe dreams

In May, after returning from a golfing holiday in Scotland, I dabbled briefly with the idea of buying a franchise for £12,500 into the "Paws and Claws" pet food organisation, but luckily decided not to pursue this as a business option...

An unsuccessful interview at Essex County Council, where the shortlist did not include my name, was followed by an equally distressing rejection at the Essex Police, and then that convinced me that applications for IT jobs were futile, and despite the efforts of the Job Centre staff to convince me otherwise, it was at that point that I gave up trying.

Hope springs

But there had already been a faint glimmer of light at the end of a very long narrow tunnel. A daring ruse at the Job Centre had gained me an interview at the local B & Q store on 3rd June, and at the interview acting dumb, I played down all of my previous career experience, almost denying any aspect of success. I simply had been made redundant, after plodding along for 17 years in local government. It worked!

The very next day I attended an induction at B&Q, and the following Monday I began working permanent night shifts, 3 days a week, as a shelf stacker, at £3.25 an hour. Only a shortfall of £20.00 an hour from what I'd been doing less than 6 months before...

Driving ambitions

Having survived the previous very traumatic year, 1994 arrived and here was a new direction.

There were 3 examinations to take to qualify as an ADI (Approved Driving Instructor), and I'd already booked the 1st one; a motoring and road craft, extension of the Highway Code theoretical exam.

From 31st January for 5 days I enjoyed a course in High Wycombe provided at my expense by my "sponsors" the Driver Training Agency, to prepare me for the other 2 examinations.

Falling off a log, it wasn't. Here was where many candidates discovered what bad or dangerous habits had permeated their driving skills over the years. There would need to be a major re-think of safe driving; but it wasn't a lost cause.

After expected success at the theory exam in London on 15th February, and a number of practice and correction sessions with the Driver Training Agency in High Wycombe I passed the driving skills exam at Brentwood on 30th March.

"Right!" I told myself, "Now for the easy bit; with all my years in training it should be a doddle to get through the next exam."

This examination on 5th May involved a role-play, where the examiner played the part of a learner driver, (too well!), and I had to provide instruction on his selected subject within the driving curriculum. This was a miserable failure; the examiner was sympathetic and helpful, and my response was inept, and insufficiently assertive...

Profit and loss

I had arrived fully qualified now in my new profession; it had taken nearly 2 years, but nobody told me what to do and when, and my success or failure depended in very large part on my own efforts.

The financial expectations would never live up to the promise of £16,000 per annum, specified in the recruitment campaign, and when Excel decided to change their franchise arrangement away from a basic percentage of work done to a flat pre-paid fee, I left them and started up on my own as Mike Haley School of Motoring...

My third trading year was going to be interesting, work was snowballing, and I was considering taking on that trainee ADI already.

None of us quite know what lurks around the corner.

CHAPTER 13

May Day May Day

"Well, I woke up in the middle of the night,
Feeling like I'd had a fright,
I said I don't feel too good at all.
You'd better take me to hospital."

Here are some more extracts from the unpublished book "Taking Chances, Making Choices". This time they cover a few days in May 1996.

LET THE HEARTACHES BEGIN

CHAPTER 13

Just a normal weekend?

Who won the Eurovision Song Contest in 1996? Was it Norway?

Nobody ever seems to remember except on those few occasions when commonsense, and a perhaps rather dubious good taste prevails, and either the United Kingdom or the Republic of Ireland win. The Eurovision Song Contest aside, I have a more important reason for remembering events that happened in May 1996.

It was a pleasant, not too chilly evening; Saturday 18th May, and we were entertaining our friends and former neighbours, Richard and Sharon, and their toddler daughter Emma.

Both Richard and myself are very fond of curries, and so it was no choice, we enjoyed another gut buster Madras, washed down with substantial quantities of good red wine, not to mention the odd lager, and soon the alcohol took effect, naturally accompanied by the usual interesting and amusing conversation and repartee.

Later, we moved to the lounge, and had the television on low volume as background. The major evening slot was occupied by that absolute zenith of family entertainment, the Eurovision Song Contest, an ideal background when everyone is sufficiently slowed down by food and alcohol. The televised contest made Eurotrash look intellectual. As usual, the section of the programme where the votes were broadcast live, from the four corners of civilisation, was far more interesting than the actual songs. Our guests left at about 11:30 p.m., and we went to bed. It was a normal night.

Upon waking on Sunday morning at about 8 a.m., I had a peculiar sensation in the left centre of my chest. It was difficult to describe, but it was like a dull ache across the top of my rib cage, a tightness, a hollow and heavy feeling, like someone had built a small pile of books on top of me which I couldn't move, and which did not change whether I was lying down or standing up. My first thoughts were that the previous night's curry was laying rather heavily on me; it was just indigestion and it would go away once the day's work got going.

I was working as a self-employed driving instructor, running a one-man school, using my own car. Sunday was always a very busy day, teaching pupils who lived in Hatfield Peveril; a village about five miles away. There were 5 hours instruction to do. After making some sandwiches for my lunch, I went off to work at about 8:50 am. It was a warmish early Spring day, there had been a little overnight rain, but the sun was shining, and it promised to be a pleasant and profitable teaching session.

The sensation in my chest was just a niggle, and it didn't really get much worse, although it varied a little in intensity. My ability to carry out the work did not seem to be impaired, and as driving instructor's days go it was a typical and successful day. There were a few serious moments, some laughter, and a few hairy scary bits. One of my pupils did tell me later in the year, that I had seemed quiet, and a little preoccupied that day.

At about 2:30 p.m. my day's work was finished, and I headed home, and looked forward to enjoying the early spring weather. We spent the rest of a summery afternoon cruising the country lanes around Chelmsford, in my Robin Hood open top kit car (a heavily disguised Mark 5 Ford Cortina). About 5 p.m. we headed home for our Sunday roast. My appetite wasn't enormous, but the roast lamb with cauliflower, carrots, and roast potatoes was memorably delicious. I didn't eat it all, and passed on the sweet.

We spent an "active" evening watching the television. The usual programme mixture for Sundays was You've Been Framed, Coronation Street, Heartbeat, London's Burning, and the South Bank Show. Good stuff for couch potatoes:

Fly-on-the-wall comedy, quality soap, light weight whimsical drama (with good 60's music), drama featuring fireman who are very seldom seen fighting fires (London's not burning, but our dinner might be), and finally culture (perhaps?).

Both Rosemary and Michelle asked me several times during the evening if anything was wrong. I had mentioned the funny feeling in my chest, and remarked that I might be coming down with the flu, and also had a slight stomach upset.

Rosemary went to bed at about 10:30 p.m., and left me to watch the South Bank Show on my own, and I still cannot remember what the subject matter was. Soon after 11:30 p.m., I also went to bed, feeling no worse, and no better. The thought never crossed my mind, that this discomfort I had tolerated all day could be anything more than trivial.

Although I found it difficult to get comfortable and felt a bit cold, my usual method for dropping off to sleep was effective. No! It's not what you're thinking; sex on Sunday night is out of the question, there is a "Y" in the day.

Lying on my back, breathing deeply, I gradually relaxed my body, and then visualised playing a round of golf on the familiar course at Bunsay Downs. This always worked for me, and usually by the time the game is halfway through, I have shot 6 pars, 2 birdies, and an eagle on the par 5 and I'm in the Land of Nod swapping golf stories with Jack Nicklaus and Nick Faldo.

At around 5 am I awoke in a cold sweat, the pain in my chest was much more intense. The small pile of bricks had now become a sleeping elephant. The sensation had spread up into my throat, and it no longer resembled anything like indigestion or a sore throat. I felt sick, and had great difficulty catching my breath. Waking Rosemary I pleaded, "I feel much worse, I can't breathe; I think you'd better drive me to hospital."

Thankfully, she didn't reply, "Come here and have a cuddle, you will feel better in the morning, let's go back to sleep, and phone the doctor later."

In a daze we both got up. Getting dressed was quite painful and difficult, especially moving my arms. I grabbed the first clothes that came to hand including a "Guns 'n Roses" t-shirt with a skull and crossbones on it.

It was still dark but quite warm for early morning, as we got into Rosemary's very reliable blue Vauxhall Nova. Driving instructor's habits are hard to break, and even at this time, only partly aware, and obviously close to unconsciousness, Rosemary received her directions to get to Broomfield Hospital, about 3 miles away. It is easy to recall negotiating the three roundabouts, and a set of traffic lights, and then I have a vivid memory of bouncing on the cats-eyes along Broomfield Road as we passed the lines of parked vehicles. My instinctive reaction to the intense pain was to make a face like a baby with colic, and gently rub the flat of my hand across the breastbone area in an up and down movement. Who knows if it helped?

As we approached the hospital entrance, the sun was rising over the green fields of Butler's Farm, stretching out along the Chelmer Valley, and that was my last memory for a while. Although Rosemary says that I told her where to park within the hospital grounds, and was able to find the A and E entrance myself, I do not remember this...

Something's gotten hold of my heart

Without any effort on my part I had become patient number 277889, but I was shortly to learn, where I was now being looked after, I would be very far from just a number. I remembered nothing at all, until the evening of the 20th May, when I came round in CCU (the Cardiac Care Unit). I had an oxygen mask on my face, contact pads stuck all over my chest and arms and legs for the ECG monitor with the trailing wires, and a drip feed tube in my right hand going to a heparin pump. Uncomfortable and confused and very hazy about what was going on, I asked a lot of questions but I couldn't seem to focus on the answers. I didn't really know where I was, even when Rosemary tried to explain what happened...

People

CCU was a mixed ward, so there were both male and female patients, with whom I shared the ward, and 7 or 8 beds in all. At 47, I was by more than 10 years the youngest patient in CCU at the time, and most of them were at least in their 60's.

My life changing

On the night of Thursday 23rd May, I had a life-changing experience.

It had been a difficult day; I had been bad-tempered, irritable and depressed. Rosemary and me had a disagreement, and I sat up in bed at about 10:30 p.m.

with pen and paper to write something down. Since my teenage years I had always found it useful to express my hopes, dreams, fears, and anxieties in the form of poetry or songs.

What I started to write that night turned out to be what I subsequently called "Knockin' on Heaven's Door (revisit 1996...)

Nobody died in real life, did they?...

Preparing my escape from a safe place

Over the next few days I made good progress, spent a lot of time talking to the other patients, and taking walks down the corridor to the TV room. I was now able to do everything for myself, including washing, going to the toilet, shaving, showering, etc. I had approval to go where I wanted as long as it wasn't outside the ward area. A lady called Julia Davidson came to see me, and put me through the acid test to see if I was fit enough to go home. This very easy test consisted of walking down 2 flights of stairs, and then walking up them, at my own pace. If this didn't feel too strenuous, or got me out of breath, then I would be fit to go home in a day or two. My cardiologist then told me that I could go home on Tuesday 28th May...

Armed with my medication, and my new instructions on what to do to change my lifestyle, I left the hospital in the late afternoon of Tuesday 28th May, after a stay of 9 days.

CHAPTER 14

Cardiac Arrest

"And when I find I'm all alone,
With just my thoughts to comfort me,
That's when I'm sure it's good to know,
To know that you're still there with me.
Beyond a shadow of a doubt,
It's clear as far as I can see,
That every step along the way,
I knew that you were there with me."

The story of Clever Clive and the Mushroom Harvest was written for a specific purpose, and for some time was lost amongst forgotten scribbles. Until, in February 2014 I rediscovered it. Having retyped it into the computer, I decided it would be a good idea to write a story around the story to illustrate why I had written it in the first place. At worst it would be an exercise in writing in the first person for a change. So this is a true story written from personal experience.

Clever Clive and the Mushroom Harvest - The Full Story

Written sometime during 1993/4, and described in February 2014

On 31st December 1992, Woodward the hatchet man with an unfeasibly obvious black wig administered his coup de grace, and made all incumbents of the management structure at the City of Westminster's Information Technology Department redundant. After 2 years of impending doom, it was a welcome relief from a system gradually misappropriated by yes men and incompetents, decaying in quality, and increasingly stagnating into a vast pool of mediocrity.

I was glad it was all over, and after 17 years service received a substantial redundancy and severance payment. The wolf wouldn't be at the door for a long time, but at nearly 44 I soon realised that I was considered too old and far too expensive to get another similar position. My professionally constructed CV was indeed impressive, but whenever the difficult subject of salary arose at all the interviews the frowns and sharp intakes of breath always indicated a "Thanks, but no thanks".

The Job centre caught up with me and I was interviewed by a juvenile snotty faced no-hoper who wouldn't have been capable of recruiting an emperor penguin in Antarctica. He advised me that I didn't qualify for Job Seeker's Allowance, but that I could try for Council Tax Benefit. After filling in the necessary forms and sending them off to Chelmsford Borough Council, I was surprised to find that we qualified for a reduced rate payment.

Six months passed, and I took up a temporary position as a non-professional golfer, and then a letter arrived. To be exact it wasn't a letter, it was a notice from the Council stating that I was in arrears to the tune of over £200 pounds which they intended to collect as a lump sum on the next 1st day of the month.

There was no problem in affording to pay up, but it was a matter of principle.

Several telephone calls over a few days were spent being shuffled between the Revenue and Benefits Sections and getting nowhere.

I kept telling them, "I gave you the information you requested. It was accurate and true. I haven't done anything wrong, and you haven't even had the good grace to apologise for your mistake."

Revenue said, "You are in arrears, and we have a right to collect it all in one go. Don't blame us, it's all Benefits fault."

Benefits said, "Your application wasn't processed properly. It's not our problem if Revenue want to collect the arrears in one go. That's the way the system works."

"Well it's not the way my system works." was my reply. The next day I went to my Midland bank branch in the High Street, and cancelled the direct debit in favour of the council. A few days after the next 1st of the month I received a letter from the council, restating my arrears and telling me that their direct debit had been returned unpaid.

In the intervening period I'd wondered how someone in less fortunate financial circumstances than me might have reacted to the council's unreasonable behaviour. Supposing you were a pensioner scraping around to make ends meet, or someone with severe problems who might become suicidal with worrying about not being able to pay.

If I remember correctly the full name of the Borough Treasurer given on the council letterhead was Clive Whitehead. I decided to write to him personally. In my letter I outlined the facts, without making any appeal to his better nature. My last sentence simply said "Please read the attached story."

"Clever Clive and the Mushroom Harvest

Once upon a time in the land on the edge of a large wood there lived a wise old giant called Clive. He was so wise and clever that everybody called him

Clever Clive. He had many children, who lived and worked together with him in a lovely big cottage which had been given to him by the Lords of the Giants in the Crown Cyril. The cottage was called the Crown Cyril Ostrich.

His two favourite sons were Rev and Ben. Rev was a tall, strong, dark-haired lad, impetuous and brash, who didn't care about anyone or anything, except the mushroom harvest. Ben was a good-natured fair-skinned gentle boy, who was very keen on fairness and justice.

Whilst Ben would be quiet and understanding in expressing himself, Rev was always outspoken and insensitive. Clever Clive loved his children, and tried hard to keep them all under control.

He, and his family, had been given the job of stock-piling the mushrooms so that the Lords of the Giants who lived in a fantasy land called the Crown Cyril would never run out.

Once a year the Lords of the Giants had a big party where they ate nearly all the mushrooms Clever Clive and his family had gathered. This meant that Clever Clive would have to send out his two sons into the woods to tell the little people who lived under the trees and bushes there, how many mushrooms would need to be picked by each of them to keep the Crown Cyril happy. Clever Clive would work out the sums, Rev would collect and count the mushrooms together, and Ben would make sure that everything was fair, by measuring the legs of the little people. This was so that those with smaller or weaker legs did not have to pick so many mushrooms. Ben and Rev enjoyed their work and the little people did not mind as long as everything was done fairly.

One day when Ben was in a hurry because Clever Clive had promised him an extra mushroom for tea, he took the magic yellow tape measure with him when he went to visit one of the little people called Sadheart, who lived under a fallen tree right in the middle of the wood. Sadheart was told how many mushrooms to pick, and because his legs were so very small he was pleased not to have to pick too many.

So, Sadheart gathered his mushrooms everyday, and sent them to Clever Clive at the Crown Cyril Ostrich.

Some time later, when Rev and Ben checked the mushroom store they found some mushrooms missing. Clever Clive was not pleased with his two sons, and told them to go away and find out where the mushrooms had gone. Rev was feeling lazy and bossy, and he bullied Ben to go out again and measure, with his everyday brown tape measure, all the little people's legs. Ben trudged into the wood and spent all day from dawn till dusk re-measuring. Sure enough, when he came to look under Sadheart's log, he was there fast asleep. So be measured his legs without waking him.

The next day Ben told Rev that there were some mushrooms missing because Sadheart's legs had not been measured properly the first time. Rev stormed into the wood on the back of his fiercest dragon, breathing fire, and found Sadheart still asleep under the log. He roughly shook him awake, and told him to go and get more mushrooms, or he, and Clever Clive, and the Lords of the Giants in the Crown Cyril Ostrich would be very, very, very, angry.

Sadheart shook with fear, and promised to go right away to pick mushrooms and to deliver them to the Crown Cyril Ostrich that evening.

Off he went in search of some mushrooms, but it had been rather cold the previous night, and there were very few to be seen. In his confused and desperate state he picked some toadstools instead.

When he had gathered as much as he could carry, he went back to his humble home and counted them.

"Oh dear ", he said," the Crown Cyril Ostrich will be very angry with me, what shall I do?"

He worried and fretted, and fretted and worried, and couldn't think of a way to keep Rev happy. He knew that if Rev got very angry he made the little people collect all their mushrooms in a huge heavy wheelbarrow, instead of lots of small light paper bags. Sadheart was so tired!

Night time was near, and poor old Sadheart was in deep despair. He ate just one mushroom for his tea and then he fell asleep under a pile of leaves.

Unfortunately, he was so tired and confused, that he ate a toadstool by mistake and later that night he died.

When Rev found out, he just demanded more mushrooms from all the other little people.

When Ben found out, he was very sorry that he had mixed up his tape measures, but he wouldn't take the blame.

And, when Clever Clive learned that Sadheart had been so worried that he had killed himself, he turned a blind eye, and just made sure that Ben and Rev would tell the same story to the Lords of the Giants in the Crown Cyril.

When the mushroom stock is short because Ben makes a mistake by using the magic yellow tape measure instead of the ordinary brown one, then shouldn't Sadheart should be told first that a mistake has been made, and second that Ben is very sorry. Shouldn't this should happen before Rev demands that all the missing mushrooms be collected.

Perhaps, Clever Clive was not so clever; maybe he didn't get the full story from Rev and Ben.

Did Sadheart have to die needlessly, because Not so Clever Clive always allowed Rev to bully Ben?

Does anybody, including Ben, Rev, Not so Clever Clive, or the Lords of the Giants in the Crown Cyril, know or care which pile of leaves Sadheart is buried under, as long as the mushroom harvest is collected on time."

A few days later I had a phone call.

"Can I speak to Mr Haley, Michael Haley please?"

"You are speaking to him."

"Good morning Mr Haley, my name is Clive Whitehead. I'm the Borough Treasurer. Thank you for your recent letter. Would you mind very much coming in to talk to me about your council tax?"

"No Clive, I think that's probably a good idea."

We arranged a date and a time, and the call was finished politely.

The following week, I put on my best suit and went to the meeting.

"Good morning. I have an appointment with Clive Whitehead."

"Oh yes, follow me Mr Haley." said the receptionist leading me into a large office with a plush carpet on the parquee floor, and quality real

wood furniture.

Clive smiled, and we shook hands, and sat down in a circle with two young ladies who represented the Revenue and Benefits Sections. They were introduced to me as mine host poured tea and offered biscuits.

"Would you like to tell us what this is all about Mr Haley." said Clive.

I repeated all my previous arguments including concern for the way the council might provoke a sad reaction from a less privileged customer.

Ms Revenue sneered her text book stance, and looked at me like I was a Tennant's super lager swigger on a park bench.

Ms Benefit smiled sweetly, but wouldn't make any admission of her department's mistake.

Clive listened, and waited for a natural pause. Then he said, "I found your letter very amusing Mr Haley, and I'm well aware that we could make improvements in the way we deal with the public. This is an unfortunate situation, and we can rectify it."

Then he dismissed the two ladies thanking them for their input.

"I think the concerns you've raised in your story are very realistic, and I thank you for bringing them to my attention in an interesting and amusing way." Clive said.

I drank my tea and took another biscuit. He continued.

"In the circumstances I think the best thing would be if you reinstated your direct debit, and we waived your arrears, which as you say are our fault not yours. Would that be OK?"

"Yes, thank you very much." I replied.

Saturday Night Flight

Adolescent experience crystallizes on a Saturday night. Boy meets girl, eyes meet, things move fast, thighs meet, and inevitably instant pleasure leads to predictable disappointment. Always intended as a song and recorded in January 2000 on a demo album called "Echoes in the Spells of Fate". This piece is a bit crude and may cause offence, but I can't be nice all the time.

Written: started 1985 and finished 1996

When I saw you at the disco last Saturday night,
Dressed just like a virgin in your perfect white,
And I saw right through your t-shirt in the ultraviolet light,
And I felt as if I could, and you looked as if you might.
I thought you were the girl for me,
But I was too blind to see.
I really thought you were the girl for me.

I had a few more lagers till I felt a bit pissed,
Then I said to myself, "It's time to take the risk."
So I boogied up towards you in a beery hazy mist
And said, what's a nice girl like you doing in a place like this?
I thought you were the girl for me,
But I was too pissed to see.
I really thought you were the girl for me.

This pathetic little chat-up line you didn't seem to mind,
So we danced a while together closely entwined,
But I really didn't know that you had something more in mind,
To get me horizontal for some bump and grind.
I thought you were the girl for me,
But I was too blind to see.
I really thought you were the girl for me.

We sped off in my dad's Cortina at the speed of light
And parked in some secluded spot at dead of night,
You said to me, "Let's get in the back." and I said, "Alright",
When you had your wicked way with me I nearly died of fright.
I thought you were the girl for me,
But I was too blind to see.
I really thought you were the girl for me.

I found out pretty quickly that I wasn't in your class,
But there I was about to get my end away at last,
"What precautions have you taken?" suddenly you asked,
I said, "It's all right 'cause I have strapped a plank across my arse."
I thought you were the girl for me,
But I was too blind to see.
I really thought you were the girl for me.

I tried to drive you home but I was pissed up to the eyes,
We'd only gone a mile or two when I was breathalysed,
I said, "Oh that fucking charming." You said, "Don't be so surprised.
One way or the other you must pay for the ride."
I thought you were the girl for me,
But I was too blind to see.
I really thought you were the girl for me.

So bang went my virginity, my poor old heart just sank,
And if you pulled that trick again I'd have to say, "No thanks!"
If that's what all the fuss is about I'd rather have a cup of tea,
Unless of course you happen to have six million in the bank.
'Cause then you'd be the girl for me,
And that's a stone cold certainty,
I'd really know you were the girl for me.

May Day May Day.

A distress signal paints a picture of a life changing personal experience. She was a stranger, but she was dying in the adjacent hospital bed, and as I watched and listened from just a few feet away I absorbed the reactions and emotions of the nurses who fought so hard to save her. The poem became a song recorded at Amber Studios in January 2000 on a demo album called "Echoes in the Spells of Fate".

Written in Broomfield Hospital, May 1996

I watched and I listened for six hours long,
but at the end of the battle, when her last breath was gone,
they'd fought to save someone that they never met,
who was trapped in the blackness of a tightening net,
trapped in the blackness of a tightening net.

Just a few nights before they'd done the same for me;
confounded the Reaper changed my destiny,
these unsung angels and heroines all,
who fight the Grim Reaper whenever he calls,
who fight the Grim Reaper wherever he calls.

Sure I always knew life was precious it's true,
but I hadn't a clue how hard they fought for you,
and if they then lost as the battle ensued,
how they cried for that someone that they never knew,
how they cried for that someone that they never knew.

Talkin' Cardiac Arrest Blues

This song was written from personal experience about the potentially difficult subject of suffering a heart attack. There is humour in the most distressing of situations. I know, because I lived to tell the tale. This was always intended to be a song in the talking blues style, and was recorded at Amber Studios in January 2000 on the demo album "Echoes in the Spells of Fate".

Written June 1996

Well, all day long I hadn't felt my best,
Had an elephant sleeping on my chest,
I found it hard to catch my breath,
I didn't know it was a matter of life and death.

I thought about what it might be;
Serious indigestion;
Influenza;
Or even, Mad Cow Disease.

By that evening I felt a bit worse,
Lost my appetite, but had a big thirst,
Had a touch of the Delhi belly,
Spent an active evening watching telly.

Same old crap;
Coronation Street;
Heartbeat;
London's Burning;
Heart of the Matter;
I got bored so I went to bed.

Well, I woke up in the middle of the night,
Feeling like I'd had a fright,
I said, "I don't feel too good at all.
You'd better take me to hospital."

Broomfield, that is;
Not too far away;
Nevertheless, better get me there
Pretty damn quick!

I got in the car and we started to drive,
I felt like a man who was barely alive;
Last thing I remember as we rode,
Was bouncing on the cat's-eyes in the middle of the road.

The wife was grateful;
Most unusual,
I didn't criticise her driving; not even once.

Well I walked into A and E,
And a moment later it hit me,
Had VF and MI,
Didn't know if I'd live to die.

Well I didn't go down no long white tunnel,
And I didn't see any angels,
And I didn't hear Aled Jones singing,
Or Kiri Tekanawa;
I survived the heart attack,
But them abbreviations nearly got me though.

Well if I'd wanted to die and leave a space,
I'd picked the wrong time and I'd picked the wrong place;
I went to the door, and I gave a knock,

And then they gave me an electric shock.

Defribulator that is;
Can't recommend it;
Just like a bolt of lightning;
 ZAP! POW!

They'd torn my favourite t-shirt off,
So I took a breath and I gave a cough;
That Frankenstein electric whack,
Had done the trick and brought me back.

Minus my t-shirt,
With two burned nipples,
And a broken collarbone.
Well, t-shirt, collarbone, nipples;
Small price to pay for being alive!

Knockin' on Heaven's door (revisit 1996)

Written following the experience of my first heart attack. A song that was never recorded. This is a poem that provided a catharsis for me. In post heart attack depression I needed to get this "off my chest".

Written July 1996

On the 20th May, as the morning came in,
I knocked on the door, but they wouldn't let me in.
I had my passport stamped and set,
But I hadn't used enough of my visa yet.
Heaven's door was slammed in my face -
I had a longer sentence in the other place.

Then I waited in the foyer for a couple of days,
And up and down the stairs some journeys were made,
As the voices of concern were expressed and raised,
The angels with no wings sympathised and praised,
But they made some inquiries and everyone was sure,
That there was no point in knocking on Heaven's door.

The mists started clearing and the reasons became sure,
Why I'd only had a quick peep behind Heaven's door.
And as the night drew in on the 23rd of May,
St Peter whispered in my ear, "They gave your place away,
Go tell your people, the angels all agreed,
We've done a full investigation, and you're not the one we need."

So I raised my spirits high, and I went to let them know,
There were many good reasons why I didn't have to go.
All they really needed now, was to try a simple task,
And give a sign of love, for which I didn't have to ask.
It had been tough for all of us, but there was one thing very sure,
It was me who had been knocking on Heaven's door.

So I chose my special person to carry out the task,
To give a sign of love, for which I didn't have to ask,
For we both knew for certain, and we were sure,
Why I'd had the opportunity, to knock on Heaven's door.
For reasons I don't understand, and I think I'll never know,
She threw the gate back open wide, and insisted that I go,
So I climbed back up the stairway and chose forevermore,
I'd prefer to take my chances behind Heaven's door.

Beyond a shadow of a doubt

At this point in my life, having learned a tough lesson about my mortality, I began to take an interest in more spiritual matters. This led me eventually to being a regular churchgoer for nearly 10 years and becoming a born again Christian. The song was recorded at Amber Studios in January 2000 on a demo album called "Echoes in the Spells of Fate". How small we all are in the great realm of things.

Written November, 1996

I laid upon a browning leaf,
Falling from a rowan tree,
And when the autumn winds they blew,
I knew that you were there with me.
Beyond a shadow of a doubt,
It's clear as far as I can see,
That every step along the way,
I knew that you were there with me.

I sat inside a pure snowflake,
That fell out of a Winter sky,
And when the cold North wind blew,
I knew that you were there with me.
Beyond a shadow of a doubt,
It's clear as far as I can see,
That every step along the way,
I knew that you were there with me.

I crawled inside a buttercup,
And slept there with a honeybee,
And when the Summer breezes blew,
I knew that you were there with me.
Beyond a shadow of a doubt,
It's clear as far as I can see,
That every step along the way,
I knew that you were there with me.

I saw the first new born lamb,
The last blue wave upon the sea;
The whispering wind it spoke my name;
I knew that you were there with me.
Beyond a shadow of a doubt,
It's clear as far as I can see,
That every step along the way,
I knew that you were there with me.

And when I find I'm all alone,
With just my thoughts to comfort me,
That's when I'm sure it's good to know;
To know that you're still there with me.
Beyond a shadow of a doubt,
It's clear as far as I can see,
That every step along the way,
I knew that you were there with me.

Shadows

I remember writing this after a late afternoon walk in the countryside along the Chelmer Valley enjoying the warmth of the sunshine.

Written in July 1996

Tall fleeting narrow shadows softly fall
And silent slowly slip across green summer evening hills.
Hills, so timelessly serene;
Unchained by greed of human needs,
Untamed by careless crude machines,
Inflamed by virgin purity.

CHAPTER 15

The Wheels Fall Off

"Sure I always knew life was precious it's true,
But I hadn't a clue how hard they fought for you,
And if they then lost as the battle ensued,
How they cried for that someone that they never knew,
How they cried for that someone that they never knew."

Here are some more extracts from the unpublished book "Taking Chances, Making Choices". This time they cover the period from May to the end of October 1996.

WITH EVERY BEAT OF MY HEART

CHAPTER 15

Taking Chances, Making Choices

Going home

Making the 3 mile journey from Broomfield hospital back home, retracing the route we had taken 8 days before, I sat in the back of Rosemary's car on a lovely, bright, warm, sunny May day. The air, despite the warmth, seemed somehow sweet, cool, and fresh, almost humid. I can remember asking Rosemary to slow down, because after the calm, relaxed, and cosseted atmosphere of the CCU it seemed that at 40 mph we were moving very fast.

As we neared Springfield, I couldn't help thinking what a beautiful sunny day it was. I had mixed feelings; happy to be alive, but still in total disbelief of the events of the previous 10 days. Arriving near home was a bit like coming back from a long holiday, where everything appeared to be little different; somehow larger and more prominent, more significant, brighter, more noticeable than the way I had remembered it.

A few minutes later I sat in my favourite armchair at home, on the verge of tears, as much tears of relief as disbelief.

"How did this happen?" I puzzled, "And why?"

There were no easy answers. I wasn't completely aware at that time what an enormous effect these events would have on my life to make it so different to my life as it was before. Probably, being back home it dawned on me that what I had experienced was a narrow escape; a salutary lesson, and a reminder that none of us are immortal, and that everlasting life is a spiritual dream outside the realms of this physical world. It was not necessarily just Nature's way of saying, "Slow down, take stock, think more carefully about the way you do things, and the way you react to or value things.". It was a lot more than that, and I was only just starting to find out.

Despite the fine weather outside, what was happening inside my brain was unpredictable. In the early days of June 1996 I started to write a humorous account of my experiences, and called it "Talking Cardiac Arrest Blues". This was quickly set to music, using a similar guitar style to Bob Dylan's, Talking World War Three Blues. Perhaps the tiniest germ of the idea for me to end up writing this book was initiated then?...

Advice after a heart attack amounted to pure common-sense, but unfortunately although it was the same commonsense message I had heard many times before, it took the shock of my heart attack, before it began to sink in that the advice applied to everyone including me.

All I had to do was adopt a healthier low-fat diet, limit consumption of alcohol, not smoke, try to steer away from stressful situations, and take exercise; nothing could be simpler, easy-peasy!

If all that was possible then I could live to ripe old age...

I was proud to be British, and didn't feel it necessary to blame my country of origin for my condition. It was a totally alien concept to me to even be able to imagine what it would have been like to be any other nationality.

So, I was now 47, but I didn't feel that much different to when I'd been 27. A little slower, a little less tolerant, a bit more fussy, but nevertheless NOT OLD!

I had grown up in a household full of women; Mum, 4 sisters, no dad. A unique and rewarding experience, only a privilege few could share with me. With perverse naivety I considered that I might understand and appreciate women from a knowledgeable perspective. How could any man dare to say that?

Women were wonderful! But they were also enigmatic, impossible to fully understand, fickle and unpredictable. Us guys were straightforward, easy to understand, knew what we wanted, we were targeted and focussed, tough and resilient, everything was so simple. The thought never dared to spring to mind to be anything less than a man...

Euro96 football

One of the major events that happened shortly after my first heart attack was the EURO96 Football Championships held in England.

The revival in England's International Football fortunes under the custodianship of Terry Venables had the whole country able to focus on believing in itself for a short while again. This at a time of immense National gloom due to the unwelcome overstay of the totally inept post-Thatcher Conservative government; staying on to the last ditch, doing the wrong things (badly), and implementing its "Money matters! People don't" policies.

For a short few weeks we were all reprieved of the gloom in the economy, rising job losses etc. It was a wonderful time of National belief.

I am sure that we genuinely believed that as hosts we could win this competition. And then of course, we came across the old enemy, now transformed as a united Germany side, who always seemed to have the capacity, with the notable exception of the World Cup in 1966, of foiling our plans and spoiling our party. The revival of the country; the belief that good times were here again however briefly, echoed my own situation where I was recovering from the biggest shock, and up to then most traumatic experience of my life. I knew this would change my life, but I didn't know at the time it would be for the better.

I followed and supported England's twists and turns of fortune through the tournament, along with the rest of the good-natured national enthusiasm. I lived through the disastrous draw 1-1 against Switzerland, to the 2-0 defeat of Scotland, the other old enemy (not only in football terms!). I was thrilled and excited; "Over the moon!" at Paul Gascoigne's brilliant solo-effort goal in that match, and then filled with amazement at the 4-1 defeat of Holland. We were unbeatable; nothing could get in our way now! Could it?

Then against Spain after 0-0 at full time, the penalty shoot-out, and who could not admire the defiance and confidence of Stuart Pearce's penalty and David Seaman's save from the Spanish player Nadal, to take us through to the battle against Germany. My nails were bitten to the quick, and I was as "sick as a parrot" as the repeat tension of another sudden death penalty shoot-out, culminating in poor old Gareth Southgate's miss, thereby allowing Germany to qualify 6-5 on penalties.

Inevitably, with bland predictability it was a boring final. Germany beat the un-fancied Czech Republic 2-1.

There was a parallel here between my own recent fortunes, and those of the England team, in that we both had to pick ourselves up and develop some new self-confidence and belief in our ability to go on to better things. Like the England team I had to continue with the revival even after the unceremonious dumping out of the competition. Like the nation I also had to carry on after distress and disappointment. I believed that my heart attack had been a little warning sign to "take-it-easy", "slow-down", "chill-out", and although I was later to be proved wrong, I didn't believe that my situation was likely to be serious...

Back on course

In a spirit of elation, I arranged my first game of golf on 19th June at Essex Regiment Golf Course just a few miles away, and although the weather was stiflingly warm, I managed to complete my target of 9 holes, about 1.5 miles, with a couple of brief rest periods, in about 2 hours. There were no worrying symptoms, no angina, and no warnings to take this rehabilitation period more easily. Perhaps it was all too easy?

Par for the course

Since I'd first become hooked in 1989, I loved golf; couldn't imagine that my life would be fulfilling without it, and dreaded the possibility of having this important activity, beneficial both mentally and physically, taken away from me. After the first game of 9 holes on 19th June, I waited until 25th June, until I was legally permitted to drive again, before I had my next round at Bunsay Downs near Woodham Walter. There are 2 courses at Bunsay, each of 9 holes. The Downs, a standard par 35, and the Badgers par 27 (9 holes of par 3's). The Downs, despite its name is relatively flat and easy walking, apart from the long up-hill par 5 hole. However, the Badgers has some steep, but thankfully short, ups and downs, and could be hard work, especially if it was warm. On this day it was warm. So I contented myself with an easy 9 holes on the Downs course, completed uneventfully. I was relieved to find that my golf stroke scores had not increased dramatically as a result of my heart problems...

Driving

Standard advice from the DVLA for cardiac patients was that a break from driving for 4 weeks was required, and it was also necessary to inform the vehicle insurance provider of the change of circumstances. My driving holiday lasted from 20th May to 25th June, about 5 weeks. I didn't find this too restrictive, because Rosemary could drive me anywhere I wanted to go...

People and places

In 1996 we had lived in Chelmsford for over 16 years, and although I knew Dr. Hariram by sight, my visits to his surgery had been infrequent. Not only did I not believe in bothering the GP with minor ailments like colds, coughs and flu, but in my early 20's I had lost faith in doctors, after I had been unnecessarily prescribed the then fashionable tranquillisers to overcome a minor nervous problem. I reasoned at that time that all doctors ever did was educated guesswork, in the process of which we were all just guinea-pig experiments, like beagles in a tobacco research laboratory, and with an equal proportion of responsibility and irresponsibility taken by the technicians for any mistakes or slip-ups made. The only time I had sought to see Dr. Hariram was when I had a serious back problem in 1991; had been laid up and off work for 3 weeks, and subsequently been advised that I had extra vertebrae in the lower back (L5) which pinched the sciatic nerve...

My Health Visitor, Nova did a great deal to cheer me up and encourage me during her 4 visits In June 1996. She was easy to talk to, and made some of my more lonely days much more interesting, and I am sure that she probably stayed on each occasion for longer than she had planned.

Was it angina or just anxiety?

On Friday evening of 11th October I was on the way home at about 8:30 p.m., after dropping Michelle off at the Dukes Experience Night-club in Chelmsford. Whilst I was stopped at the traffic lights between Victoria Road and Springfield Road there was a strange and acute prickly sensation in my chest. It was like someone was repeatedly digging the point of a sharp pencil into the area just left of my breastbone. I was frightened!...

Family problems

Rosemary had been working for the Community Hospitals Group for seven years, the last two as an Assistant Chef at the Lawns Nursing Home in North Springfield. During my stay in hospital and immediately afterwards, Rosemary had taken time off work, but when she returned to work things did not go well. Far from being concerned about her state of health and sympathetic about our situation, her employers showed no compassion whatsoever. With the awareness that she had been to the hospital herself for investigations into a repetitive strain injury in both wrists (carpal tunnel syndrome), caused by the nature of the work she did, they attempted to make her feel guilty that she had taken the time off to look after me. They dared to suggest that she had let her working colleagues down. Her annual assessment during July reflected this lack of appreciation of her efforts, and little understanding of the stress she had been put under by my illness...

Treadmill test

On 22nd July 1996 I had a "treadmill test" at Broomfield Hospital.

The purpose of the treadmill test was to assess the heart function under increasing, although not intolerable, physical pressure. It involves walking on a rolling road whilst being connected to a continuous ECG monitor.

To begin with the simulated road was flat and moving slowly. But gradually the machine was tilted to simulate walking up a hill which became progressively steeper. The nurse advised me that the test would take 12 minutes, and if I suffered no ill effects in this time then everything was fine.

Unfortunately, at about 11.5 minutes the experts gathered around me, pointed out something untoward on the ECG screen, and stopped the test...

Travelling and holidays

There was quite a large amount of travelling and holidays in the period between May and October 1996. My GP had sanctioned holidays, as a good way of relaxing, and had provided the necessary written permission to fly required by the airlines. He was probably not aware that the things that I liked to do on holiday didn't necessarily fit exactly with the advice I'd been given.

The last thing I tended to do on holiday was relax!...

Working again as an ADI

Once I began driving again, the next step naturally, was to re-embark upon my employment as an Approved Driving Instructor (ADI).

I resumed this work on 13th July, but my customer base had shrunk from 24 pupils to 10. This was partially due to the pupils, once started, preferred to carry on uninterrupted in their tuition, and partly the need for some of them to continue lessons immediately before a driving test which I'd already booked for them.

A gap of 7 weeks in my availability may not have been good for them, but it was disastrous for the one-man, one-car business I was running.

With my remaining loyal customers I only had about 10 hours work a week, and this was not enough to provide a living; and it was difficult to acquire new customers because of uncertainty about the future. I had the expectation then that my future as an ADI was in serious doubt...

Relate

Rosemary and I attended Relate counselling once a week on Tuesdays from January to September 1996. They didn't wave a magic wand, but they did teach us how to communicate better, and how to better understand each other's needs within a relationship. Undoubtedly the counsellor, a very patient and clever lady called Jackie, saved our marriage. The prevailing situation in our marriage was, at the time, just another obvious indicator of the overwhelming stress in our lives, which I believe was still a hangover from my redundancy in 1992...

Angiogram day

October 21st 1996 was a grey, damp day. Upon waking I had already fasted for 12 hours, and duly obeyed my instructions by only drinking a small glass of water with my medication. The train from Chelmsford at about 7 am reminded me of the many years I had commuted to London to work - lots of very rude people pushing and shoving, impatient to grab seats. It made me feel glad that I no longer needed to do this, and the lapse of 4 years seemed like an age away. After arriving at Liverpool Street, the Underground service to the nearest station; Barbican, was just two stops. However, choosing to walk provided a nostalgic reminder from the Sixties when I last worked in this part of London, even though an enormous amount of redevelopment had changed many aspects of the area. Walking via Moorgate, Finsbury Square, and London Wall I eventually found the hospital complex...

At about 4:30 p.m. my cardiologist, Dr Dawson appeared. He explained that what the angiogram told the cardiologist (in pictures) was precisely where there might be blockages or narrowings of my coronary arteries.

I thought he would say, "Well, Mr Haley, there is nothing much to worry about." Then, with a reassuring smile he would add, "If you lead a decent life, little drinking, no smoking, careful diet, lots of exercise, I might see you again when you're 80-ish."

I was surprised, shocked and devastated when instead, Dr Dawson, albeit very gently said, "We have found one or two problems, and you will need a little operation."

There was a reassuring smile, as if to say "Sorry!"

I am not ashamed to say I cried...

My state of mind from May to October had been fairly normal, but after the angiogram I felt understandably down and depressed.

CHAPTER 16

Every Silver Lining has a Cloud

"The days were long and I felt fine,
I played golf from time to time,
Today, tomorrow and the following day,
I felt fine there was golf to play."

Here are some more extracts from the unpublished book "Taking Chances, Making Choices". This time they cover the period from the end of October 1996 till late November 1997.

Taking Chances, Making Choices

CHAPTER 16

WILD THING, YOU MAKE MY HEART SING

A bright spot

One of the other patients in Bart's the day of my angiogram, was a gentleman called John. His condition had been deemed so serious that he had to stay there, and await immediate surgery. What a pleasant and unexpected surprise when I bumped into him again at the cardiac rehabilitation Christmas Party at Broomfield hospital in December 1996. He looked much better; he was tanned and healthy, showed me his scar, and we had a lengthy discussion about the operation and recovery period, which was very reassuring...

I love Paris

On Friday 7th December 1996, we went on an extended trip to France to celebrate our wedding anniversary; Rosemary and myself with our friends Kay and Pete., After the Dover/Calais ferry we drove the 120 miles to a town called St Quentin, (not San Quentin as in the Johnny Cash song), staying for two nights in the Hotel De La Paix.

The following day we made the sentimental journey into Paris to see the sights, and then returned the 100 miles or so to St Quentin, and enjoyed a celebratory dinner in the hotel. On Sunday we returned to Calais and visited the hypermarket on the way home. A well organised set of different interesting activities. There was very little strain in the travelling which was done at a leisurely pace. We spent the whole day in Paris and saw all the sights, the Eiffel

Tower, Notre Dame, the left Bank, the Champs Elyssee, Place de la Concorde, Place de L'Etoile, journeys on the Metro, etc. Upon return to the hotel we looked forward to our evening meal...

Hasta la vista baby!

For one week from 6th January 1997 Rosemary and I were on an all-inclusive holiday in the hotel Honolulu, in Magaluf, Majorca. Our first experience of all-inclusive resulted in predictable excesses. During the holiday, the weather was absolutely terrible, mostly quite cold with very frequent rain, and this tended to confine everyone to the hotel, making the ultimate excuse for even greater excesses. All meals were buffet style, where you could eat as much as you liked of what you liked, and all local drinks including soft drinks, beers, wines and spirits were also free of charge.

Human nature being what it is, sampling everything, and being greedy, seemed to be acceptable. Free drinks very few people can resist.

I leave it to your imagination.

Putting it to the test

It is interesting to note that we returned from Majorca, on 13th January, and it was on the 21st January that I had my first cholesterol test. Who knows whether the excesses of our holiday had any bearing on the result? After having a heart attack in May 1996, I did not have a cholesterol test until January 1997. A routine meeting with my GP resulted in my first cholesterol test, and the result was 8.2, and he immediately put me on a cholesterol lowering medication called Simvastatin. He explained that despite being on an apparently healthy diet, and taking more exercise, and limiting alcohol consumption, (Ho! Ho!) that the cholesterol level might just be a result of the way my body worked as a factory.

After 6 weeks I had a further cholesterol test, my level was down to 5.2, the doctor was delighted, but insisted that I should stay on medication for the foreseeable future. Cholesterol was therefore an area that was totally under control by medication, was easily monitored, and no longer provided any significant risk factor to my health? A successful change easy to undertake by just prescribing one tablet a day...

Golf and guts

For about 5 years running in April or May of each year, I had been on a golfing holiday for 3 to 4 days, with some colleagues. Initially we travelled to Scotland for these holidays, which included playing both Carnoustie and the Old Course at St. Andrews, but after that became too far to go, we switched to South Wales. In 1997 we were making the second visit to a hotel called Bryn Meadows Golf and Country Club, near Blackwood, South Wales, from 16th to 19th May 1997. This was a 5 crowns Welsh Tourist Board approved hotel quite close to the town. Blackwood is the pot-noodle centre of the known universe due to the location here of a Golden Wonder snack foods factory. The hotel has its own golf course and the attraction is just this.

The Welsh holidays always started Friday and finished Monday with one competition round each day, and optional additional rounds for anybody who had the energy. Having it in mind that only a week or so after my previous visit to Bryn Meadows I had suffered my first heart attack, I resolved to take things as easy as was possible in the circumstances. I only played 18 holes each day, and created for myself the illusion that I was relatively sensible with the eating and drinking. Kiddology was by now a practised art form.

On the way home we attempted to play a golf course in Malvern called the Worcestershire. Unfortunately, it was pouring down with rain, and feeling completely exhausted by the previous 3 days golf and 19th hole excesses, I felt decidedly unwell and fed-up. Clearly this extra game was too much for me, and I gave up after 15 holes...

The doctor sent me for blood tests at Broomfield hospital, and as a result, I was asked to attend the clinic of a Urologist, Dr Tassadaq.

On 10th July 1997 an ultrasound scan discovered that I had what the urologist called a lazy kidney. He told me not to worry as was quite common.

I had a further test in the department of nuclear medicine at Broomfield Hospital on 24th October 1997, which involved me lying on the bed perfectly still for about 40 minutes while photographs were taken of my kidneys. Some radio-active contrast was injected in my arm and passed through my system. This test determined that my right kidney had no function whatsoever, but also that my left kidney was performing brilliantly. Nobody could say how long I had been working on one kidney; it could have been from birth, or perhaps I injured myself either as a child, or later as an adult...

Five years before I had been in a highly paid job, successful in my chosen career, and living the good life, and here I was now with my health ailing on the number of fronts; no job, unable to work, little money, and who knows what future. This made me feel worthless for a while; depressed and anxious about the future. However, it is not my nature to let things like this drag me down for too long. In the words of the well-known song, only a few days later "I picked myself up, dusted myself off, and started all over again."

The French Connection

Over the 29th/30th October 1997, once again we were on an extended day trip to France. This time Rosemary and I went with my sister Marion, and her husband Geoff. Leaving on Saturday, we stayed overnight at the Holiday Inn Garden Court in Calais, and returned on Sunday afternoon. As you have probably guessed by now, the evening meal in the hotel involved copious quantities of alcohol. Once again I enjoyed several beers before, several bottles of wine with, and several beers afterwards. That was another 20 units all in one day. Did I have any idea, or was I just being stupid?

The Great Pretender

I diligently went about the business of improving and increasing the exercise regime immediately after my first heart attack. In August of 1996 we acquired a dog, and I then therefore had no excuse not to go for walks. However I did invent the excuse that he was a small dog and only needed small walks. I found out eventually that this was not necessarily true.

As soon as I got to a basic level of fitness, my exercise regime tailed off altogether. I relied upon one thing and one thing only, for my exercise regime, and because we all tend to fall back to something that we feel comfortable with, for me this was obviously golf...

I played golf as frequently as I possibly could, sometimes playing three times in the week, and even when the scores were going badly, I still enjoyed it.

I had grown past the stage where I got annoyed with myself for achieving high scores, so this potential stress factor no longer applied. When rounds went well and I was playing below my handicap this would result in a feeling of euphoria.

Someone said, "A bad day's golf is better than a good day dying."

I certainly attempted to live up to that. But, I was kidding myself that golf was all I needed...

They also serve?

After phoning Dr Dawson's surgery to advise that I would like to be added to the waiting list for surgery on 29th October, and then confirming this in writing a few days later, a few weeks later, I checked with Dr Dawson's surgery to make sure they'd received my letter.

I received a letter from Dr Dawson to tell me that I had been referred to a cardio-thoracic surgeon; Mr. Gareth Rees on 29th November 1996...

In September I was also advised that it was unlikely that I would have my operation before December. In an acutely self-interested question, I asked myself, "Why does no one worry about me; does anybody care?"

The answer was "NO! Not much!"

Swings and roundabouts

The stress of work had vanished, because I could no longer work as a driving instructor, and so no longer needed to worry about earning my living in a stressful job. But this created other stresses. Increasing stress at this time was the financial worry of having to get by on Rosemary's part-time salary, the residual redundancy payment from 1992, and my Incapacity Benefit.

I had been paid this benefit from January 1997, starting at £47 per week, and gradually increasing to £62 per week. For many years, from December 1992, we had been falling back financially to my redundancy money and other savings that we had accumulated during our affluent period. But now this nest egg was dwindling, and getting close to critical...

Spiralling down

All the ignorance of necessary lifestyle changes and excesses of continuing bad habits acquired in my good life were now beginning to take a more significant and recognisable toll.

My health had deteriorated in a number of ways. So, on 15th October 1997 I visited my GP. All of my appointments consisted partially of mutual updates on developments of my overall case, and partially of a "How do you feel at the moment?" report.

I advised Dr. Hariram that my by-pass operation was now scheduled for December at the earliest, and also of my urologist's examinations, and my next step on 24th October. But, the main subject was how I felt.

I reported my latest set of symptoms in detail. Frequently, I was waking up feeling dizzy or drunk, and had occasional chest pain and breathlessness, (although to me it didn't seem to be anything like angina). Also sometimes there were what I could only describe as "flutters". There was difficulty with the urgency and frequency of passing water, I seemed to feel the cold acutely, and the gaps between my migraines were becoming shorter. Dr. Hariram was sympathetic, but he probably knew that I had been overdoing it, and offered only reassurance that things would soon be better.

Bring some good news

It sounds like the whole of this period was depressing and going steadily down hill. But I didn't have to work, and could do almost exactly as I wanted every day. I had to ensure that I did not laze around doing absolutely nothing; that I had both mental and physical stimulation. There were times of depression, feeling low, feeling sorry for myself.

What did I do to keep myself going?

The result of this was that I decided that I needed to dedicate more time to re-learning, and developing playing the guitar, and singing. From then on I made a lot more effort not only remember words and chords, but to develop some repertoires, and to learn how to play a lot better. In this process I completed the writing of about 30 songs, some of which I had began writing over 20 years before. My interest in a varied number of styles to music has been rekindled. This after many years of stagnation. During the following period I began to write the next bit of Talking Cardiac Arrest Blues up to the point where I got the result of my angiogram.

Every cloud has a silver lining, and every silver lining has a cloud

On the 5th November, (which may have some quirky significance?), I received a letter from Bart's saying that I was now at the top of the list for surgery, and asking me to attend the hospital for pre-surgery tests on 2nd December. This would be in preparation for my surgery which would be on 8th December.

When I received this letter two emotions clashed with each other, and all of the worries of the waiting were brought sharply into focus. All at once I was elated, pleased, even excited about the prospect of getting my surgery at last, but at the same time the fears of what was about to happen came to the surface. If it is possible to be at once relieved and also apprehensive then I was that. I thought about going into hospital and making a full recovery, and also about dying during the operation.

I did not know that fate was about to deal me yet another card from the bottom of the pack before this date, and not many days ahead!

CHAPTER 17

Cri de Coeur

"Life is hard and then you die!"

Here are some more extracts from the unpublished book "Taking Chances, Making Choices". This time they the period from early November to early December 1997.

Taking Chances, Making Choices

CHAPTER 17

CRI DE COEUR

Vive la France!

At about 8:30 p.m. on the evening of November 7th 1997 I set off from home with my golf clubs in the back of the car to go to Thundersley, where my nephew Nicholas lives. Here I was to spend the night, before setting off early the next morning together with Nick, my brother-in-law Brian, and "nephew-in-law" Robbie to play golf in France at a new golf course called Golf du Bois de Ruminghem. I expected to be back within 24 hours, but there was a big surprise waiting for me...

It was a quite fresh November morning; not too cold, dry, and with good visibility on the road. We had to be at Dover at about 6 am to catch the 7 am ferry to Calais. It was still dark but sat in the back of the car, it was comfortable...

It was going to be an interesting crossing!
There was still no warning of what was to come!
After a short while we loaded onto the ferry; quite a small vessel of the Stena Line called Pride of Kent, old, but having been refurbished to a reasonable standard. We made our way to the self-service restaurant, where we all ordered the Full Monty English breakfast...

As we pulled into the car park at the golf course, I felt a little tired, not used to getting up at 4 am, but the seasick feeling was beginning to subside. The car park was empty, and so was the clubhouse, and we therefore expected to have the golf course to ourselves.

As the ground was a little damp we all decided that we would carry our golf clubs, instead of having the difficulty of pulling a trolley. All excess golf paraphernalia was ejected from the bags, and we made our way to the clubhouse to check in. We were greeted by a large blonde Dutch lady whom I was later to find out was called Saskia. I was eager to get started.

Doing a Bing?

The first hole was a par five, with a lake on the left. I felt sluggish, but this was not unusual for the first few holes of a game, and we were not in any hurry. I had 5 layers of clothing on to make sure I stayed warm, tolerating the restriction in movement. We finished the first hole at a leisurely pace, and I scored 8.

"Not too bad a start!" I thought...

On the second hole (a par 4), I hit a good tee shot, and a good 2nd, and completed the hole in 6. By this time, I had noticed that carrying the golf bag seemed to require an enormous effort. But nothing else occurred to me, except that I began to wish I had used my trolley...

So, after 3 holes, I was 3 strokes adrift from my handicap. But I was enjoying the course and the golf, and I was looking forward to completing the round in something less than 105.

"You will get going in a minute, and things will come better", I told myself.

As we walked to the 4th tee I began to feel dizzy, disoriented, and distinctly unwell, but I still put it down to early morning tiredness and the after effects of feeling seasick. My tee shot only went about 80 yards into the right hand rough. But this was only short par four, and I was confident I could recover and score 5.

When I picked up my bag it seemed to weigh 4 tons. It was then that it sprung to my mind that this perhaps was something more serious than just tiredness.

After 4 attempts I managed to hit the ball from the rough, but by that time I was in bad trouble. As I went to play my next shot, it suddenly felt as if someone had kicked me in the chest. I felt breathless and weak, and I knew that there was only one thing that this acute stabbing pain to the centre left underneath my ribcage could be...

I pleaded to my golf colleagues "I don't feel very well!", and sat down on the damp grass and took a couple of puffs from my GTN spray. Brian had become most concerned. After a few seconds, it was clear I needed urgent medical attention...

Brian picked up his golf bag and mine, and heading in the direction of some small white buildings, we started to make our way back. It was an enormous struggle for me, I was in intense pain and unable to capture any oxygen...

We struggled together to within 50 yards of the club house, but by then the pain and breathlessness was so intense that I could not continue up the last little incline.

Brian rushed into the buildings and requested them to call an ambulance. A green keeper came out to me as I was lying on the edge of the first tee and put a blanket around my shoulders, and helped me the last few yards into the building. Saskia sat me down and gave me a glass of water, and quietly reassured me "Don't worry; the emergency services are on their way."

It was obvious that this was another heart attack and not just a severe bout of angina, the pain in the left centre of my chest was overwhelming, and I could not catch my breath. I was feeling cold but sweaty under my five layers of clothing.

I sat slumped over the table gasping for every breath. My body felt like it weighed 10 tons. I could not feel my arms, or my legs. My head felt like a lead balloon...

Since my first heart attack I had sometimes wondered whether I would "Do a Bing Crosby." Apparently Bing, who was a keen golfer, had just left the 18th, and entered the clubhouse saying "That was a very good round of golf", and with one last beaming genial smile had experienced a heart attack, and died...

Soins Intensifs

Upon arrival in Le Centre Hospitalier de Calais, I was taken to the 4th floor to Service de Cardiologie et Soins Intensifs. In the Soins Intensifs there were 4 bed positions, I was quickly surrounded by 6 medical personnel, at least 4 of them doctors in white coats with name badges on the front, all labouring away exchanging pieces of paper, and discussing what had happened, what treatment I had received in the past, and what was going to happen now. My schoolboy French could not cater for understanding all of this...

Lost in France

Then, Brian and the boys went home, and I was then left on my own in France, feeling very lonely and abandoned, and knowing that it was very unlikely that I would see any visitors the next day, (Sunday)...

On Sunday 9th November I awoke in a bed in the Soins Intensifs of Le Centre Hospitalier Calais, after a very uncomfortable night, little sleep, not much care and waves of discomfort...

Chez Nous

I awoke to the sound of church bells ringing, but leaning up in bed was unable to see the church across the car park from my hospital window. Perhaps, it was because I couldn't see much of what was happening, it reminded me of when I was in school. In French lessons we read a magazine called "Chez Nous", (Our House), dealing with everyday life in a French town.

I imagined all the people on their way to church, dressed in their Sunday best; the women in their hats; men in their best dark blue wide pin-striped suits and shiny shoes. The children, smiling and excited as they had always been in "Chez Nous"; dressed for the occasion. I imagined the whole family inside the church singing hymns, obviously in French, but nevertheless instantly recognisable as holy songs...

The day could not go too quickly, I looked to Monday, and the expectation of some visitors. Meals came and were eaten, but I don't remember what they were, eating them in a semi-conscious daze and dropping off to sleep frequently because there was little else to do. It was a merciful relief when it got dark and the late afternoon arrived. I had some phone calls, but my personal line was not set up yet. So far, no one who was able to speak more than a few words of English had presented himself or herself to me.

Some time mid-morning one of the nurses, seeing that I was bored and depressed brought me some magazines to read.

These were French (obviously), but what a Godsend!

Rattle those pots and pans

A good night's sleep followed on Sunday night only because of the lack of proper recharging the previous night. In a sense I crashed out.

I had started to work out how to ask for things that I wanted; the first of which was a pee-bottle, followed shortly after by a bedpan. I don't really know if got these requests right, but the responses were appropriate. I had no trouble with "Je voudrai un boutelle." But asking for a bedpan lost something, (or perhaps gained something), in direct translation. I could ask for "Un casserole du lit" but that is "a casserole of the bed". I don't think people do "their business" in saucepans, even in France?

What I needed was "Un bassin du toilette".

Schoolboy French is unlikely to equip anyone for a stay in a French hospital in critical circumstances...

My visitors brought me my Walkman, some music tapes, some golf magazines, and a French phrase book. At least I would now be able to occupy myself. Their morning visit was very short, and they went off to the golf course at Ruminghem to see if Saskia was there, and to thank her for everything.

These visitors returned again in the afternoon for another short period, by which time I had regained possession of my bed. They promised to visit me as often as possible, and to organise others to visit. I felt guilty that I had caused so much upheaval for so little benefit in visiting time.

A room with a view

Later that afternoon I was moved to another room away from the car park and church bells which had provided my amusement for the previous period.

The new room was on the opposite side of the Hospital building, facing the canal which gave the hospital its address on the "Quai du Commerce". From this room I could see the canal and the road which ran either side. In the middle distance I could see a bridge with a large red-painted metal frame, and further away I could just make out some buildings, and cranes, in the port of Calais, and some way off, traffic moving on the motorway. In the middle distance the bell-tower of a church was visible. Later I discovered that this was the 13th century mixed Tudor and Gothic style church of "Notre Dame", which had been the place where a certain Captain Charles de Gaulle married his sweetheart Yvonne Vendroux in 1921...

Another day, another room

On Tuesday morning I was walked up the corridor to an examination room, where some X-rays were taken, and I had a conversation with a cardiologist who spoke a little English. I suppose that I had become attuned to listening to French, because conversation with this doctor using his rudimentary English, and me my rudimentary French, did not seem too difficult. By now, in a limited "subscriber" sense, I had become something of an expert on heart matters, and I was able to point out to the cardiologist whereabouts in my X-rays the problem was likely to be with my coronary arteries. When I left this examination room the nurse guided me back to another room where in the meantime they had moved all my possessions. It was still on the canal side of the hospital building, but a few yards further away from the port of Calais. This was the final room that I would stay in Calais Hospital, allowing me to continue with my survey project of French traffic and driving habits...

Bedside manners

Nurses varied from totally disinterested to wonderfully charming and stayed in their categories throughout my stay...

Some did not want to know, and others were quite happy to sit with me for 10 or 15 minutes, and have personal conversations about my family, or theirs, or how I came to be there. What a delight when someone took the time to have a sensible non-medical conversation, and in return I was often able to ask for their help in getting my phrases or pronunciation correct...

For some of the time that I was there I had a Heparin drip located in my right arm, just the same as in Broomfield. But when this was removed they administered Heparin injections twice daily in the stomach. One of these injections was usually given at night, at about 2 or 3 in the morning.

Some nurses were careful and sympathetic, offering a few words of reassurance before applying gentle pressure after finding suitable spot, and would try their best to make me comfortable before administering the needle. Having a needle put in the stomach can never be pleasant, but if I was tense and not relaxed it obviously hurt more.

With others, it was vest-up, grab lump of skin, and puncture it, squeeze, and goodbye till next time. Sometimes it was like the Birdseye peas advert "Sweet as the moment when the pod went pop."

One nurse in particular, whose name I do not have, but was wearing a badge indicating she was married (Madam not Mademoiselle), was positively rough. She would enter the room banging the door, switching on the light and saying in a very loud voice "Wake up Monsieur 'Aley." She would then just grab a bunch of skin in the stomach area and stab me with the needle before beating a hasty exit almost as quickly as she had come. No smile, no care, no conversation, no TLC. Thankfully this did not happen too often…

They gave me some literature about the hospital, which gradually became easier and easier to understand, as I read it 4 times a day. This booklet combined with my E111 form, and some information relating to medical care abroad which I had from a travel agent, clarified for me what would be expected to happen as regards payment for my treatment, and also gave me useful information as to what questions I should ask, what papers I would need etc., before being discharged…

I fully expected that I would need to pay the "Journalier Forfait", that is the daily "Hotel" charge for non-medical things like food, keeping the room clean etc., before I left. This amounted to the exorbitant sum of about £7.50 per day. I allowed myself a chuckle, thinking that despite the austerity and Spartan aspect of the surroundings this was true bargain, and given the opportunity I might stay here again instead of at the £30 per night B & B at the Holiday Inn Garden Court just up the road. But then again, maybe not!

Home is where the heart is

On Tuesday 18th November, I was discharged from hospital, with medication, and a letter for my GP. My condition after this heart attack had deteriorated. Now I couldn't walk more than 50 yards without being out of breath and in need of a sit down or rest. I didn't feel very confident about undertaking anything more physical than going to the bathroom.

Brian came to collect me about 10 o'clock and I had already packed (a supreme effort, which needed a 30 minute lie-down to recover). We waited for the papers to arrive and then we were free to go. I had been in Calais Hospital for 10 days, from 8th to 18th November...

The journey continued, and at last we arrived in Chelmsford.
Little did I know that the worst of the whole nightmare was about to begin.

No heart for the job

While I had been away, Rosemary had been busy. She had not been able to sleep for worrying, and so had set about decorating our dining room. I couldn't help but comment, that the room looked very grand and regal, but at the same time subdued and peaceful like a "chapel of rest".

My GP, Doctor Hariram, made a home visit on Wednesday 19th November, carried out a thorough medical examination, discussed what had happened, took his time, reassured me, and then did his absolute best to help me get the attention I needed.

I was physically in very bad condition; the 2nd heart attack had done substantial damage to my heart muscle and reduced the amount of blood and oxygen that it was receiving. I was unable to walk more than a few yards without extreme fatigue, breathlessness and sweating, couldn't walk up the 14 stairs in our home, without 3 rests, and had no energy or stamina whatsoever...

Unfortunately, there was a complete unwillingness of the Health Authorities to understand my situation. My cardiologist and Bart's Hospital, whom

Rosemary had been in daily contact with, seemed to be incapable of assessing my needs, and expediting my admission to hospital for surgery. Waiting around to see whether the various offices of the Health Authority were interested in saving my life, it seemed they were not capable of coming to any decision, and there was little evidence of any attempt at liaison, We repeatedly came up against brick walls, or went for hours a day down blind alleys, only to discover and re-discover that nothing seemed to work...

Unchain my heart

An appointment with Dr Dawson, was arranged for the following Wednesday 26th November. It had taken 9 days from returning from Calais, to getting me into Dr. Dawson's surgery, and even this appointment seemed to be reluctantly and hastily arranged at the last moment the day before.

Sitting in the Broomfield Hospital waiting area, we saw him enter the building, perhaps returning from lunch, with a very large file under his arm.

Mine? I don't know!

I imagined a chain of events where Simon Burns had prompted David Johnson, the Chief Executive of North Essex Health Authority, into action to make sure that Dr. Dawson saw me as quickly as possible.

Whether this actually happened or not, I do not know, but it comforted me to imagine that it did. If your MP can't carry any weight, who can?

Dr. Dawson examined me in his usual calm and reassuring way, but reassurance wasn't enough. I needed positive action. He was only able to tell me "I will see what I can do, but I can't promise anything." He even explained, to my total horror, "This heart attack may have done sufficient damage to your heart that we will now have to wait until things settle down again before we can consider surgery". I left his consultation in utter despair, in tears, unable to put any understanding into my predicament. I was totally convinced that I would die, and nobody would care. But worse was still to come!...

Rosemary and myself were so upset after the visit to the cardiologist, that we went together to see Dr Hariram on the evening of 27th November, to plead again for some relief from this torture. Sadly, having reached the limits of his authority, he was now dependant on Dr. Dawson to get me admitted to Hospital. We left his surgery feeling even more depressed.

How and when would this spell be broken?

Did anybody care?

Down in the mouth

That evening was rock bottom. I was distraught!

Then, light at the end of the tunnel!

It was agreed on Friday 28th November, that I would be admitted to Bart's on Tuesday 2nd December at 10:30 am.

During this period we contacted Anne Fitzgerald, Features Editor of the Essex Chronicle, and she became interested in our story, as an ongoing theme of highlighting the huge amount of problems created within the Health Service by growing waiting lists and dwindling financial resources.

It was to be nearly 2 months later, on January 23rd 1998 before the Essex Chronicle ran a story titled "Lives put at risk protest", complete with a photograph of me and Rosemary, which featured the cases of myself and a Michael Rowson from nearby Little Waltham...

"Life is hard and then you die!" I believe is an old Jewish saying?

At times this saying appeared to be ringing true.

CHAPTER 18

Heart in the Right Place

"A stranger's just a friend you do not know"

Here are some more extracts from the unpublished book "Taking Chances, Making Choices". The chapter has been split into 2 sections to make it more manageable, and the 1st section covers a period in early December 1997, up to a critical day in my life.

Taking Chances, Making Choices

CHAPTER 18

HEART IN THE RIGHT PLACE

Admission

The first snows of the winter fell on December 2nd, not blanketing the land like some picturesque Christmas card scene, but creating a dreary semi-darkness day, and appalling driving conditions. Lack of preparation, expertise, or practice at dealing with sudden weather changes, is a typically British trait when snows suddenly lay on the road thickly enough to make a difference to the way everyone drives. Just to add extra interest it was to be Rosemary's first attempt at driving in London. We left Chelmsford in good time at about 12:30 pm, in order to arrive at Bart's at about 2:30 pm.

I was to be admitted to Bart's for an angiogram the following day, and then expected to have my surgery on the 8th December.

I had never driven or been driven up to Bart's Hospital before, although I knew it was in the Barbican/Smithfield area just north of the City of London. So, we drove in the direction of the City of London, and then made our way towards Smithfield, thereby finding Bart's by trial and error. After the 2 hour drive we found a parking meter bay immediately outside the main entrance.

I put £6 in the meter, to pay for 3 hours parking, and then realised that the meter was taking the money, but not registering any time, nor coming up with an "Out of Order" sign. Since we were already late, we decided to leave a note on the windscreen explaining what and happened, and then rely on the goodwill of the traffic wardens. We entered the hospital grounds; found the Queen Elizabeth 2nd building and then Harvey Ward on the 4th floor.

245

The building inside, was L-shaped, with the long side as you enter from the stairway, and then a change of direction to the right, with the nurse's station at the far end. I remember thinking that this was not good security practice, and that anyone could wander in and terrorise the patients.

We reported to the nurse's station and were asked to wait in the day room, which was at the elbow in the corridor. In this room, decorated with curtains and pictures on the wall, there were about 8 comfortable chairs and a television with remote control. Various people came and went through this room in the next two or so hours; some of them in normal dress, and some in pyjamas and dressing gowns. I assumed that other people were being admitted to hospital that day, but just as when I had attended this hospital for my angiogram, patients didn't speak to each other. They only spoke, if at all, to the people who accompanied them, or alternatively just stared blankly into space. To be quite honest, there was very little to say.

Several times I went back to the nurse's station to remind them that I was there. Each time they promised to deal with me in a few minutes. As the parking meter time came close to expiry, I suggested to Rosemary and Michelle that they might like to go home and leave me. As soon as they went, and I was left on my own, a nurse came to the day room and took me to my bed, which was in the best position in the ward, right at the end of the corridor, so that I could see all the comings and goings.

Outside in the cold, dark winter afternoon, the traffic wardens had completely ignored the note on the windscreen, and not bothered to ascertain whether the meter was working correctly or not. They just issued a ticket, which I felt in the circumstances was very insensitive.

A stranger's just a friend you do not know

Now I had my bed, Beverley, a pretty, and elegant West Indian lady, with a very pleasant manner and disarming smile, attended to some paperwork with me. We completed a questionnaire giving my personal details and an outline of my health history over the previous few years. I mentioned to Beverley that I had recently been in Calais Hospital after a 2nd heart attack. Beverley then asked me to get into my pyjamas and dressing gown. I took my Walkman from my bag, inserted an Eric Clapton tape and lay upon the bed, and Beverley went over to the other side of the ward to talk to a lady patient.

After a while, as I was floating away to the music, I realised that Beverley was pointing and waving in my direction. I stopped the tape, and went across the ward, and was introduced to a short, blonde, lady in her late 50's. June came from Mawney Road in Romford, and to my surprise she had been in Calais Hospital at exactly the same time as me. She had also suffered a heart attack on a day trip to Calais, and had subsequently been admitted into Bart's for a valve operation a few weeks ago. We swapped reminiscences about our various experiences of the Calais Hospital; good things and bad things, comparisons with Bart's, and lamented how the French hospital staff had not sought to put us in touch with each other. Nevertheless, I did talk to June a number of other times throughout her stay, until a few days later she went home looking fit and well.

The evening meal came along, and as expected the food was just about palatable, although barely recognisable as something that humans might consider eating.

As night came, I was given my medication, and before lights-out I was advised that there was only the possibility that I would get my angiogram the next day. In preparation for this possibility, I would not get any breakfast the next morning, and would be allowed just one small glass of water with my medication.

Another day, another angiogram

I slept reasonably well, but awoke early on the morning of 3rd December, and heard the clank of the breakfast trolley making its way along the corridor. I helped myself to NO BREAKFAST, had my glass of water with my medication, completed my bathroom business, and then prepared for a dull day waiting to see if I would have an angiogram.

I was able to spend some of the time in the day room, and beginning to feel more comfortable with the surroundings I began to talk to some of the other patients.

I discovered then that Harvey Ward had 2 classes of patients. There were those patients waiting for either surgery or an angioplasty or angiogram. (The Angiogram Ward was open weekdays 8 till 6, but not at weekends.).

Then, there were those patients who had been through surgery, had spent some time recovering in Vicary Ward, and had then experienced some difficulty or some other associated problem, and been transferred back to Harvey Ward.

So, there was a lot of information to be gathered from the various people there that would be useful to me in understanding what was about to happen. Altogether the capacity of the ward was about 24 beds, and these were arranged so that the more attention or observation a patient required then the closer to the nurse's station the bed would be. At the end section of the ward, where my bed was, there were 8 beds. The whole area was Spartan, utility furnished, unwelcoming, and had that unpleasant hospital odour of cheap disinfectant mixed with human waste products...

I knew exactly what to expect, and so I lay still, and ensured that if my nose itched I would ask for it to be scratched. The doctor gave me an injection in the groin, and then made the incision in my femoral artery, inserting the little tap that would stop me bleeding. This was not painful. The small tube containing the dye was then passed up to my heart, and I watched, as I had before, on the X-ray machine which was above my head on the left. The process took a little longer than a normal straightforward angiogram because once again they had to find the Scottish doctor who has done the investigation before, so that he could find his way into my physiologically differently built coronary arteries. The primary verdict from the angiogram was that there appeared to be significant differences between the images produced by the first angiogram and this one...

Ups and downs

I began to go through the stages of getting on my feet. I started with sitting up and waiting, then swinging my legs over the edge of the bed, and again waiting for a minute or 2, before placing my feet on the floor. After pulling the curtains around me I continued with taking the operating gown off, being careful not to flash my bum to anyone. When I started to put my pyjamas and dressing gown on, having been through all these necessary steps as slowly as I could, I found my pyjama bottoms uncomfortable and I realised I had put them on back to front. So I dropped them to the ground and then stupidly tried to kick them up towards me with my right leg.

The artery burst open and blood was spurting in every direction. I pressed the attention button for the nurse about 15 times in 10 seconds in my panic, and after about half a minute a nurse casually stuck her head around the curtain and said, "Yes, Can I help?"

My distress was obvious, but she casually asked me to lie on the bed, now naked of course, and applied pressure to stop the bleeding. After 10 minutes the bleeding stopped, and a senior nurse came over and told me I would have to lie still for at least two more hours. I was not pleased. I laid back listened to the Walkman, and with difficulty ate my evening meal whilst lying down…

Hopalong

The first patient I talked to was a tall thin gentleman, built rather like myself and aged about 50. He looked pale and drawn, and not at all well. He seemed to have a great deal of trouble moving around, was in pain all the time, and floated about like a ghost. About 3 weeks before, he had apparently been preparing to go on holiday to Spain, and had suffered a sharp pain in the chest while be was getting the cases out of the loft at home. With no previous experience of heart problems, he did not know what they pain was, and as is common put it down to bad indigestion. Like most people, he could not recognise angina very easily.

Then he had sat down, had a cup of tea and began to feel better. He finished getting the cases out of the loft. Later that same evening, after a similar pain in the chest, which subsided after about 5 minutes, he had again dismissed it as indigestion or a pulled muscle…

Talking to the unkindly christened Hopalong didn't make me feel confident, but he had my sympathy.

Stop your tickling Jock

There was an old fellow in the end bed who we all called Jock. He had one of those wrinkled up and weathered faces and looked as if he might have been a naval man. Now in his Eighties, he had been admitted the previous day with difficulty in breathing, and spent most of his time on an oxygen mask, or on a nebuliser. He'd had a bypass operation some 7 years before, and a subsequent valve operation about 3 years ago, and be took everything fairly philosophically. In his previous visits to hospital he had contracted "the hospital bug", MRSA, and so he needed special treatment. However, he was lucid and able to speak clearly, and told us some great stories about his previous life....

Jersey Wingebag

On the right of my bed, was a "gentleman" in his seventies, from Jersey, whom I found it extremely difficult to relate to. From the bandage on his chest I could see that he had had bypass surgery, and he was clearly the "ward moaner", who never seemed to be satisfied, and could not come to terms with his condition. He had some difficulty in motivating himself to come back to a normal life. After a few days he was flown home, and was replaced by a lady whom I never had the opportunity to talk to...

Mr. Chips

In the end bed on the right was a middle-aged, large, tall man, whom I noticed never ate any of the hospital food. His wife was at his bedside from dawn till dusk every day bringing him breakfast, lunch and dinner. At mealtimes she went out and bought some sort of takeaway. I noticed that amongst the takeaways were such things as sausage and chips, pie and chips, Chinese food, and sometimes a curry. I wondered how he could contemplate eating all that fatty unhealthy food whilst lying in a hospital ward after a serious cardiac operation. But he wasn't the only person that I would encounter in the hospital who was unable to take all the good advice about diet and lifestyle as seriously as they should. To sit in a hospital and eat lots of chips seems to be a waste of National Health money and resources.

Florence

When June had gone home, they had put a lady called Florence, in her bed. She lived at Station Road, Shenfield; a place I knew quite well. Florence was a very sprightly and active lady in her late seventies, and the first time I noticed her presence was when she was on some kind of a machine that was making her wretch. In the many conversations I had with Florence, we were able to discuss common experiences about the area in which she and I had lived. She told me, that even at her age, she had recently bought a new Ford Fiesta car, and once a week she drove along the M 25 to Hertfordshire to see her sister...

Antipodean Betty

This lady was replaced on my left, by someone who reminded me of my German grandmother. It was not that she was German, indeed she couldn't have been less so. She had lived most of her life in New Zealand, but was now living with her son and his wife in a cottage in Four Ashes near Stansted Airport in Essex, another place I knew well. Betty, was in her eighties, and came to the ward from the post-operative Vicary Ward. At first she was very ill, having difficulty breathing, and not being able to keep any of the food down. She was unable to walk, and for a few days was confined to bed.

Something that it was necessary to get used to in hospital, was trying to eat a meal whilst people around me were vomiting or using a bedpan, or being treated in some disgusting way. Without getting used to this, I would probably have starved to death.

At nearly every mealtime, Betty would be vomiting in the bed alongside mine. Of all the people that I met in hospital, she was the one that I will remember with the most affection. A really lovely lady, who took all that could be inflicted upon her totally in her stride, never asked for any special treatment, and had the quietest and friendliest manner imaginable...

Goodbye and Good Luck

One of the difficult things to reconcile was that patients going for surgery would leave Harvey Ward, and it was unlikely that they would be seen again. This was not because of any morbid reasons, but simply because post-operative patients, unless they had some problem, would go to Vicary Ward before being discharged...

Everyday life

On the afternoon of 4th December I had a very brief visit from Dr. Dawson, my cardiologist, who advised me that the surgeon, Mr. Rees would have a chat with me in the next few days about my forthcoming operation. He did not have any information as to whether my operation would go ahead on schedule on 8th December, but I felt confident that whilst I was occupying a bed in this critical ward, that possession being nine points of the law, I would not have to wait too long. Fingers crossed, and the surgery would go ahead as scheduled anyway...

More lonely hearts

Roy Valvejob

Another gentleman called Roy had been waiting for 10 days in the hospital for a heart valve operation. He'd had a bypass operation three years before, and unfortunately had contracted a virus, which he said, "had started to eat away", at one of his heart valves. It was therefore necessary for him to renew his membership of the "Zipper Club", and for the surgeons to operate on him again and replace that valve. He had spent the previous six months having all his teeth fixed, because there was the possibility that decayed teeth would spread bacteria into the bloodstream, which would affect the function of the heart valves. Roy he seemed to be very philosophical about it. I suppose, he'd already been through a depressed stage about his health condition, but was now back to thinking that the new operation was a necessity...

Surgery Eve - To be or not to be?

Sunday 7th December was our 23rd wedding anniversary, and of course I had no opportunity to nip out and get a wedding anniversary card.

Rosemary did not seem to mind, and she visited me with a nice card during the day. This was an easy day, even though it was potentially the eve of my operation. Nothing much happened, apart from the many visitors, and naturally they all wanted to see me before I would have the surgery the next day.

At lunchtime with all the other gentleman patients, I had watched a repeat of the Big Match on the TV. This was the 1981 Cup Final replay between Tottenham Hotspur and Manchester City. As the 100th Cup Final the event became known as the very entertaining classic "Ricky Villa" final.

Villa, the Argentinean striker had been off-form and substituted in the first match which had ended as a 1-1 draw. But in the replay he became the star with 2 goals, including the memorable 77th minute solo effort. The tremendous match ended with a Spurs victory 3-2, which was thoroughly enjoyable (even for a Hammer's fan!).

From the sublime to the ridiculous! Afterwards was a film, called "The Green Berets", starring an ageing John Wayne film in one of his best "God Bless America" roles, saving the Yanks from loads of stupid little yellow men with very good weapons and no brains. This was one of the most boring starts to a film that I had ever seen, but by then more visitors had arrived, and we went back to my bed.

At about 7 p.m. that evening, a nurse gave me some industrial strength hair removing cream, which I had to spread over my breast bone and the insides of my legs from ankle to thigh. Because there was the possibility of me being operated on the next day preparation was made in the normal way. I was amazed at how effective this hair removing cream was. After spreading it on, and waiting about 6 or 7 minutes, I was able to remove hair that had been there for over 30 years simply with a piece of tissue dampened under the tap.

Later in the evening a young man, a cardiac specialist, came to see me to discuss the operation. He had me a little worried, because he started quoting at me the risks and percentages of failures involved in having such surgery. When I told him that I also had a problem with one of my kidneys, he seemed to double the risk to me. It didn't make me feel any better, and I felt this was totally unnecessary.

He advised me that I was not definitely having surgery the next day, (I was fifth on a list of four), but I needed to be prepared, and would have to wait the next day without food or drink just in case they had a slot.

By this time, I had begun to accept the two possibilities. Either my operation would be on the next day, or I would have to wait until the following Thursday, which was the next day that Bart's was contracted to carry out heart surgery for Essex Health Authority. Neither alternative was totally acceptable, but having the operation the next day was marginally better...

Cabbages and Kings

December 8th came, and surprisingly I awoke from a very refreshing night's sleep, and had not laid on the bed staring at the ceiling all night worrying about what was to come...

How could I prepare myself for dying if I'd volunteered myself into the risk of doing so, especially as I knew that if I didn't take the risk I would probably die anyway?

Comparisons with a firing squad at dawn are not valid, because with that there are no Ifs, Ands or Buts!

I gave Rosemary information about where important papers were, and how she would receive a lump sum and pension for the rest of her life.

She cried! Naturally!

I also specified 2 favourite songs that I wanted at my funeral.

The first of these songs was "It takes a lot to laugh, It takes a train to cry" from the album "Highway 61 Revisited" by Bob Dylan. This is a classic blues song, lamenting some loss or condition. It has been a favourite of mine for over 30 years, and I am sure that whenever I go to meet my maker I will still want this to be played at my funeral.

The second request concerns a song by The Eagles, written by Don Henley and Glen Frey. The song says something that I cannot say in a million words.

There is no obscurity in the lyrics, like there is in the Bob Dylan song. The lyrics relate to the way I see myself, in an allegorical sense, and I feel that they hit the button, smack on target.

In this song, called "Desperado", the desperado is me, and this only goes to show that I know myself better than anybody thinks I do...

CHAPTER 19

Resurrection

"Well I had six more days at Heartbreak Hotel,
Before they put me in hospital,
When I arrived at my destination,
More than ready to have that operation."

Taking Chances, Making Choices

CHAPTER 19

HEART IN THE RIGHT PLACE

Braveheart

The motivation at this stage was absolute and immense. Rather than feeling gloomy and apprehensive or on the verge of a nervous breakdown about what was going to happen, I felt elated, relieved and assured that I would be all right. I didn't see any possibility of anyone in this position ever getting up off the trolley and running out of the hospital in their surgical gown, with their bum flapping in the breeze, screaming "No!, Leave me alone, I'm not doing it!".

As I left the ward everybody wished me good luck, much as we had all done to the previous patients who had been taken for their surgery during the week before. I don't know how much the injection in the backside relaxed me, but one of the peculiar things was that I found it strange that I felt so at ease. I thought I would be more nervous. I expected that I would be like someone who is about to run over a line of hot coals in bare feet. Far from it!

Even after all the waiting since admission and during the previous part of the day this was one of the easiest parts of the process. I felt less tense than I had for the 2nd angiogram. I had the good wishes of everyone, and one of the things that buoyed me up was the thought, rather morbid though it was that if anything happened to me I would know nothing about it. The people left behind; Rosemary and Michelle would be left to deal with the consequences.

To me, this experience was a bit like being Nick Faldo walking down the final fairway at the Open Golf Championship towards the 18th green with the crowds cheering wildly on both sides. Waving and doffing his cap, he knew that all he needed to do to win was to get par. He would then win the tournament and the money and there would be a tremendous sense of relief.

Outside the lift I said farewell to Rosemary and Michelle, and I can remember enacting something from Only Fools and Horses. I was Delboy saying, "It's not Goodbye Rodney, but Au revoir!"

Delboy would have got it wrong as usual, and said "It's not Goodbye Rodney, but, Cafe au Lait!"...

What seemed to happen then was that the mask went over my face, and the gas did not seem to have any effect. However, when the injection was given I sensed that something like purple gas was released from the side of the mask. This is pure fantasy. It did not happen!...

Staying in ITU

When I came round I felt as if I had been born again. I was floating and I had no pain; and I was very comfortable and warm just like a newborn baby. I was aware of the various wires, monitors and leads, the mask on my face and a tube down my throat. The lines that had been inserted in my wrists in the preparation room had gone. I had an ECG monitor and the contact pads on my chest, an oxygen mask on my face, and the main line in the right hand side of my neck. However, none of these things caused me any discomfort or grief. At various intervals there was activity around my bed, but it was dark and I was not conscious all of the time, drifting in and out of sleep. When I was awake I could not see very well because I did not have my glasses. I did know that I had dressings on my chest, on both my legs, and that I was completely naked.

Rosemary and Michelle, and Mark visited me briefly in the Intensive Care Unit. Rosemary whispered something about playing golf soon, and told me later that I shrugged my shoulders, and that the nurses interpreted this as me practising my backswing. The main line in my neck became uncomfortable as I became more aware, and the two nurses attending to me would fiddle with it every now and again, to either remove something or add something to the cocktail of drugs that I was being administered.

My eyes felt very sore and gritty and I had what I can only describe as two "grow bags" under my eyelids. During the previous few hours it is certain the Sandman did not bring me any dreams, but he left me with 2 huge mounds of sand in my eyes. These could not be removed by poking about, and I was given 2 eyedroppers, one for each eye, in order to clear this up.

The worst of my fears to do with the operation related to the tube down my throat connected to the facemask. To begin with this did not feel as distressing as I had expected. The machine which performed the breathing for me during the operation was no longer in evidence, and I was breathing for myself. But I could feel the tube in my throat pressing on my windpipe.

The thought of this was perhaps worse than the real situation.

During a period of activity by the nurses, in which they fiddled again with the mainline, one of the nurses brushed against the mask, and moved the tube slightly towards the right; possibly only 1 or 2 millimetres. When this was dislodged, I began to feel uncomfortable, because it was pressing on one side of my throat. So I attempted to move it back again. The nurses misunderstood my intentions, and assumed that I was trying to remove the mask and pull the tube out of my throat. As I could not speak, I could not tell them that I just wanted to make a small adjustment, and move the mask back slightly to the left...

I was asked if I would like an ice cube to lubricate my mouth and throat. It was actually a sliver of ice, but I hadn't had a drink for the whole day, and was dehydrated from the anaesthetic. The tube down the throat put pressure on this area, and so the ice sliver was the most gorgeous lubricating, refreshing sensation cooling my mouth and throat.

Without any doubt, this was the best drink I had ever had in my life, better than any pint of beer. I was not content with one ice cube, and probably had 3 or 4. Not long after, I was offered a cup of tea, and this was another wonderful sensation. Tea had a really beautiful taste even though I was drinking it through a plastic straw from a plastic cup...

Staying in HDU

In HDU there were 4 beds, 2 occupied by other patients, and one empty space, and me. The drugs and the trauma of the operation did not allow me to be totally aware of everything that was going on, so I tended to have snippets of awareness. Despite not having my glasses, I was able to focus long enough on the name badge to find out that my nurse's name was Catherine. But because my brain was fuzzy, and my concentration span poor, I annoyed her several times, by calling her Caroline. I lay in bed for a while, and then Catherine told me that I would be allowed to sit up. Because I was still attached to an ECG monitor, still had the catheter in my bladder, and two large tubes draining my chest underneath my rib cage, this was a major event...

In the afternoon I had a visit from the physiotherapist, Sarah Rowe, a pretty pony-tailed, blonde-haired, well-built young lady with one of those jolly smiling faces and bright blue eyes. She began to teach me how to breathe, and in doing so, to clear the after-effects of my operation from my lungs. One of the exercises involved breathing in 4's. What I had to do was, breathe in to a count of 4, to a point just comfortable, hold the breath for a count of 4, and breathe out for a count of 4. This helped re-inflate and clear the lungs after all the punishment they have suffered in the operation and immediately after. Having learned how to do this exercise I was encouraged to do it several times a day. This felt like each time I could breathe a little deeper. At first, my breathing was very shallow, because there was a tight pressure across the top of my ribcage, but I breathed just a little deeper than it as comfortable to do each time I did the exercise.

I had no more visitors that day, but continued to attempt to have a conversation with the gentleman opposite. We would pass three words, and then nod at each other for the next 10 minutes. I fell into a fit-full sleep, and then early in the evening Catherine helped me back to bed. I was now becoming aware of some aspects of my body, in particular the prominence of my heart beat, and the totally dead feeling across the top of my chest. Catherine finished her shift, and the night shift arrived, and sadly the special care of the High Dependency Unit vanished with her...

Paracetamol worked as a painkiller, but the euphoric effects of morphine had held me in seventh heaven. With Sweet Sister Morphine, I had been hang gliding from the top of Angel Falls in Venezuela for just over one day, with all the feeling of euphoria and excitement you would expect. On Paracetamol, I now landed on the hard rock on the jungle floor with an enormous bump...

Moving on

Although I was well wrapped up in a dressing gown, and with the blanket around me I noticed the different sensations of warmth and cold as we passed from HDU to the lift well, into the lift, out again on the 3rd floor, and into Vicary Ward. This was particularly noticeable in my legs. Being able to sense changes in temperature so dramatically was a reassuring sensation. It told me that I had all my organs, particularly my kidneys, working properly.

With my possessions in a bag on my lap I was taken to my new location, which was a small private room where I was helped to stand up out of the wheelchair. Catherine then said "Let's put you into the bed so that you can have a rest."

I felt very grateful to this young lady for making me feel so comfortable and well cared for in my time in HDU. So, spontaneously, I gave her a big kiss on the cheek, and gratefully said, "Catherine, you are the best nurse I have ever been fortunate enough to be looked after by."...

Staying in Vicary

The nurses arrived and administered my drugs. I had my menu cards again and could order my meals. The room was cold compared to HDU, and the windows had lots of drafts. There was a bed, a bedside table, a wash basin with funny taps, a wardrobe in the wall and an armchair that was not very comfortable and not very welcoming. I thought perhaps someone had died in here, but then again that was silly, 100's of people had probably died in there. I wished I were back on morphine and out of it. This was the first time I had felt cold since before the operation, and had needed to control my own body temperature. I shivered from time to time and worried if my one good kidney would stand up to things OK. The weather outside was cold and windy, but there was some condensation on the inside of the windows, so it must have been warmer inside. Below the window was an area that looked like a children's playground, but there were no children on this cold winter's day. The cold seemed to concentrate the heavy tight feeling in the top of the chest, stopping me taking a full deep breath...

One of the things that could cause distress, but was unlikely to cause any worrying injury was sneezing. Because of the way this made the chest fly out and back in quickly, it was best to stifle any sneeze by tickling the roof of the mouth with the tongue, or blowing the nose until the "I want to sneeze" sensation subsided. If the worst happened, and I couldn't stop the urge to sneeze, I prepared by holding the towel firmly over the chest, and then let it go as forcefully as was comfortable.

Something held in great dread, of all these little natural body reactions, was hiccoughing. Thankfully, this is usually the result of eating too fast, and taking in too much air at the same time. Eating is not something I had any desire to do. My appetite was wafer-thin, and my food intake was like an anorexic sparrow...

The great escape?

On Saturday morning, I woke up with a smile, thinking "Right! That's my last night in here."

An Aussie nurse, Michelle, came after breakfast to perform a final little operation on me; to take out my stitches that had been pulled tight to hold the wounds created by the drain tubes in the middle of my chest. I was alarmed to see her wielding a bare blade scalpel so close to my skin and over such a sensitive spot. But she used it skilfully and quickly and there was minimum discomfort. After that, I went off for a supreme effort of taking that first shower. I stripped off and turned the shower taps on, and as I went to lift my left leg into the shower, I noticed some blood around my ankle. Not a serious spurting of blood, like when I'd been recovering from the angiogram, and broken my femoral artery open, but enough to make me concerned. I pulled the attention cord, for the nurse, and then sat and waited for her, depressed, upset and nearly in tears...

I slowly packed all my belongings away, looking forward to my escape. During the packing, the phone rang for me at the nurse's station, and when I returned it rang again at the opposite end of the corridor. I'd nearly finished packing when I had another call at the nurse's station again.

I was worn out and I needed to rest again. I got up on the bed and lay still; I was sweaty, breathless and felt as if I was overheating. Then it started.

Not the prominent and by now comforting sense of the heart thumping away in regular pattern, not the head throbbing, or heart in the mouth sense of palpitations. No! This was different!

My heartbeat felt like I was on a trampoline, one minute furiously and frantically jumping from floor to ceiling and the next flat, lifeless, as if not beating at all. I was frightened!

I thought "Oh Shit! I'm so near to going home, and now I'm going to die."

I pressed the attention button for the nurse, several times, and at long last Aussie Michelle appeared. "You don't look too good, Mike", she offered, "Tell me what's happening?"

I described what was happening. I was panicking, but they told me to keep calm! They wheeled in an ECG monitor, and stuck the familiar pads on my chest, and took 2 readings, a few minutes apart. My heart was still trying to escape from my chest and leave me there. The nurses were very matter-of-fact about it, and soon my friend, the smiling Chinese Doctor arrived, looked at my readings. Chuckling as usual he declared, "Oh dear, Mr. Haley didn't you want to go home?", and then added "You've got atrial fibrillation, (AF), its not serious as long as we treat it, we'll give you some medication."...

If at first ...

The next Sunday morning was 14th December and I was going to make sure that today my escape was successful. There was no way I was going to repeat Saturday's fiasco. Early in the morning I'd got the big grin from my eternally jolly Chinese doctor. He was still at work from the previous day. The doctor gave his permission for a second escape attempt, and I was ready to go. This time, I played it all down, stayed calm, and rested listening to my walkman.

During the morning I bumped into another of my fellow HDU patients; the one I had attempted a kind of semi-conscious, nodding dog conversation with a few days before. He had already been home for 2 days, and was returning for a check on the fluid in his lungs. I was disgusted to discover that the personal space that he occupied carried a strong and unmistakable stench of tobacco smoke, and despite his lung congestion and persistent cough, he felt no need to curtail his unhealthy habit.

I reflected whilst resting on my bed, The hospital ward was stark, hard, drab, dreary, and inevitably depressing, but every day miracles were performed in there. People left patched up and equipped to continue their lives. The nursing staff, set apart from the unquestionable special talents of the surgeons and cardio doctors, were just ordinary people, living ordinary lives, having the same worries, the same hopes as anyone else; earning a wage, paying bills, paying a mortgage, bringing up kids. But within that they possessed extra-ordinary qualities of patience, compassion and understanding. And, all the time, they were just interacting with a conveyor belt of strangers who came and went on an endless cycle, of life and sometimes tragically death...

The temperature in the hospital, despite variations from area to area was generally quite warm, and there I was with jacket, scarf and hat on, feeling a rush of cold air as I stepped into the lift, and moments later walking out on the ground floor. Rosemary and Sylvia held me up, while Derek went to get the car, and then I walked outside into the winter air, which seemed so cool and refreshing. They helped me into the back seat. I needed a rolled up towel to stop the seat belt rubbing on my chest scar, and then I burst into tears. I felt strange and somehow remote from everything.

Raining in my heart

When the car moved off, the throbbing of the engine provided comfort, for the first time in days, by drowning out the overwhelming exaggerated sense of my heartbeat, submerging it into the sounds around me...

CHAPTER 20

Escape from the Great Impasse
"Yesterday's a distant valley where I spent some time,
Today's a rugged mountain that I still have to climb,
Tomorrow is a winding trail that chance or choice embraces,
And time is a mysterious river running through these places."

Talkin' Cardiac Arrest Blues (Full Length Version)

Here is a return to a talking blues written from the personal experience of being a cardiac patient. After experiencing 2 heart attacks and by-pass surgery and then managing to live to tell the tale, I extended the previously recorded song. The short version was recorded in January 2000 at Amber Studios on the demo album "Echoes in the Spells of Fate". This full length version continues the story and has been performed a few times but never recorded.

Written originally in June 1996, and completed January 1998

Well all day long I hadn't felt my best,
Had an elephant sleeping on my chest;
I found it hard to catch my breath.
I didn't know it was a matter of life and death.

I thought about what it might be;
Serious indigestion,
Influenza,
or even, Mad Cow Disease.

By that evening I felt a bit worse,
Lost my appetite, but had a big thirst;
Had a touch of the Delhi belly;
Spent an active evening watching telly.

Same old crap,
Coronation Street,
Heartbeat,
London's Burning,
Heart of the matter,
I got bored,
So I went to bed.

Well I woke up in the middle of the night
feeling like I'd had a fright,
I said, "I don't feel too good at all,
you'd better take me to hospital."

Broomfield that is,
not too far away,
Nevertheless you'd better get me there
pretty damn quick.

I got in the car and we started to drive,
I felt like a man who was barely alive.
Last thing I remember as we rode
was bouncing on the cat's-eyes in the middle of the road.

The wife was grateful.
Most unusual!
I didn't criticise her driving;
not even once.

Well I walked into A and E,
and a moment later it hit me;
Had VF and MI,
Didn't know if I'd live to die.

Well I didn't go down no long white tunnel,
and I didn't see any angels,
and I didn't hear Aled Jones singing,
or Kiri Tekanawa.
I survived the heart attack,
but them abbreviations nearly got me though.

Well if I'd wanted to die and leave a space
I'd picked the wrong time and I'd picked the wrong place.
I went to the door, and I gave a knock,
and then they gave me an electric shock.

Defribulator that is,
Can't recommend it,
Just like a bolt of lightning.
ZAP! POW!

They'd torn my favourite t-shirt off,
So I took a breath and I gave a cough,
That Frankenstein electric whack,
Had done the trick and brought me back.

Minus my t-shirt,
With two burned nipples,
and a broken collarbone.
Well, t-shirt, collarbone, nipples -
Small price to pay
for being alive!

When I came round in a Coronary Care bed
I knew I was alive, but I felt like I was dead.
I couldn't recognise anyone,
but at least that elephant had upped and gone.

Been replaced, by snakes and ladders,
Wires for monitors, tubes for drips,
Aspirin, Heparin, Streptokinase, Oxygen and GTN spray,
and the mask on my face -
in case anyone recognised me.
In CCU there's TLC,
Lots of drugs and ECG's,
Lots of nurses there to please,
and an endless stream of lukewarm tea.

Yep! It's the universal cure all.
Had a heart attack?
Have a cup of tea!
You'll feel much better then.
Go on, you know it makes sense.

Pretty soon they were giving me advice
all about diet and exercise,
all about stress and cholesterol,
giving up smoking and alcohol,

I told 'em to close the barn door;
that horse is long gone,
Anyway, in my case it's hereditary.
Thanks Dad!

Fully advised and feeling better,
Soon they gave me a discharge letter,
Said, "Don't you come back here no more.
Now pack your bags, there's the door."

I went home; it was a sunny day,
Ate loads of fruit and vegetables,
No steak and chips.
Took long walks,
Didn't smoke or drink,
Slept a lot,
Didn't drive, avoided stress,
Couldn't play golf,
Nearly died of boredom!

Two months later, free of stress,
they called me in for a Treadmill Test,
"We'll speed it up as you go along.
If you do 12 minutes there's nothing wrong."

I did eleven and a half and
they weren't happy,
They said I'd need an Angiogram.
I told 'em I already had a stereo system.

The days were long and I felt fine,
I played golf from time to time,
Today, tomorrow and the following day,
I felt fine there was golf to play.
Now sometimes when I didn't play,
I just dreamt about it,
And sometimes when I did play,
It was more like a nightmare.

Well, I went to Bart's for the Angiogram,
Enjoyed it all, didn't give a damn,
Till the man came round for the consultation,
Told me I needed a by-pass operation,

I didn't believe him,
So, he said it again,
Told me not to worry though,
There's a 12 month waiting list.
I didn't feel so bad then.

Well a year passed and I got older,
Autumn came, and it got colder,
then one day just by chance,
I was out there playing golf in France,

That old elephant came back again.
This time he kicked me in the chest.
I was upset -
I'd only played four holes.

Well I laid down on the clubhouse floor
adding up my handicap score;
Teams of medics all around,
Trying to get me safe and sound.

Well I didn't pass out, or faint, or vomit -
I felt every needle,
gasped for every breath.
I wasn't much help!
I was too busy
looking for a long white tunnel,
trying to find a band of angels;
I thought I caught a glimpse of Aled Jones.

Well, I ended up in a hospital bed,
I knew I was alive, but I felt like I was dead,
I couldn't understand anyone,
But at least that elephant had upped and gone.

Been replaced, by snakes and ladders,
Wires for monitors, tubes for drips,
Aspirin, Heparin, RTPA, Oxygen and GTN spray,
And a mask on my face,
So that's no-one would recognise me.
Looks like deja-vu.
What do you expect in France?

Ten days later feeling no better
they gave me a discharge letter,
Said, "Vous ne retournez pas encore".
Now pack "votre baggage, il-y-a la porte."

I went home; it was a cold day,
Had no appetite,
Not even for steak and chips,
Couldn't walk more than a few yards,
Or climb stairs,
Couldn't sleep,
Couldn't drive,
Fully stressed,
Still, I'd waited 12 months now,
It would be my turn soon.

Confident I was top of the list,
Eight days later I saw the cardiologist,
He looked and he sighed, and he too'd and he fro'd,
And he said go home, we'll let you know.

I said thanks for your time Doc,
I feel much better now,
I'll try to get back home before I die,
Don't want to clutter up your surgery,
I know, perhaps I'll have a nice cup of tea!

Well I had six more days at Heartbreak Hotel
before they put me in hospital.
When I arrived at my destination,
I was more than ready to have that operation.

So, I joined the Zipper Club,
and, lived to tell the tale.
Could be a good idea for another song -
Let's see!
Mmmm, Talking Zipper Club Blues?

Lost

So what's this all about? Your answers may or may not give you all the clues you need. But I doubt we are asking the same question. Through it all there is LOVE! A poem that became a song recorded at Amber Studios in January 2000 on the demo album "Echoes in the Spells of Fate".

Written 22nd February, 1998

Yesterday's a distant valley where I spent some time,
Today's a rugged mountain that I still have to climb,
Tomorrow is a winding trail that chance or choice embraces,
And time is a mysterious river running through these places.

Narrow trails have brought our quest to a crossroads with no sign,
The road ahead is damned or blessed so many hills to climb.
Where is the bridge that we must cross to stand on solid ground?
For in this moment we are lost by the instant we have found.

Whilst rust encrusted hinges swing trapdoors to and fro,
Between the places we have been and those we've yet to go,
Thin doors of opportunity for moments remain open, and
Snap shut so quick behind us the instant they are taken.

There's but one path to chart this course though there are many stations,
And all is clear we steer towards one constant destination.
For many are the trials of life and many are its glories,
And chances to glance back in time for each to tell their stories.

Along the way delayed by pain, grief, consternation, stress,
Sometimes we suffer at the hands of things that bring distress.
From opposites our tortuous routes our common journeys spin,
In truth we know there's one way out as there was one way in.

Why try to bind us both with love's elusive secret treasure?
We are not then, we're only now, but we will be forever,
For love is all that can stand tall, for love provides the measure,
When we are just then, no longer now, we will still be forever.

Ballad of Luke, Jude and Nancy

If I'd been a Wild West hero, then I'd like to imagine that I'd have been a "gun slingin', gamblin' man" going down in a blaze of glory just like Jesse James. In those tough times even white girls would have had good reason to sing the blues. A poem that became a song recorded at Amber Studios in January 2000 on the demo album "Echoes in the Spells of Fate".

Written 22nd February, 1998

Luke was a cool and handsome dude,
A gun slingin', gamblin' man,
With his fancy suits, and snakeskin boots,
He rode out of Cheyenne,
He rode out of Cheyenne.

Miss Kitty was a whore in Wichita,
So well she played her game.
They never knew her real name was Jude,
The dudes, who paid and came,
The dudes who paid and came.

Luke was slick with that bottom card trick,
Aces high and smokin' guns,
Fast guns and sharp cards across the West,
Tried to end his winnin' run,
Tried to end his winnin' run.

Every day at sundown, the boys rode into town
To get their whiskey kicks,
Them roughnecks came from miles around,
To buy one of Miss Kitty's tricks,
To buy one of Miss Kitty's tricks.

Down at the Crazy Horse saloon,
When gamblin' men came to play,
Luke the dude met a gal called Jude,
And she never made him pay,
No, she never made him pay.

Bordello born, Luke's baby girl,
As the midnight moon came round,
In an ambush trick Luke bit the dust,
They shot that cool dude down,
Yes, they shot that cool dude down.

She grew up poor but she grew up proud,
Mamma died when she was thirteen;
She knew for sure where she was headed for,
The same place her mamma had been,
The same place her mamma had been.

Now when times got tough she made just enough
With cards, and bars, and booze,
And folks rode in from miles around
To hear Nancy sing the blues,
To hear Nancy sing the blues.

Molly Brown's Blues.

The movie "Titanic" was released in 1997. It was an epic film, a great story, and impacted on the imagination of many people including me. So this little song is my tribute to Molly Brown, one of the few heroes of the tragic disaster, but I am also using her and the phrase "maiden voyage" to illustrate a metaphor for learning from our errors. The song was recorded at Amber Studios in January 2000 on the demo album "Echoes in the Spells of Fate".

Written May, 1998

One day we set sail
On the maiden voyage of the Titanic,
Disaster is unthinkable,
The ship is unsinkable,
Icebergs are harmless,
Lifeboats superfluous,
We will survive,
Nevertheless, I'd hazard a guess.

That day we set sail
On the maiden voyage of the Titanic,
The vessel invincible,
To think the unthinkable,
Icebergs are due,
Lifeboats too few,
We might survive,
Nevertheless, I'd hazard a guess.

If again we set sail
On the maiden voyage of the Titanic,
It's fearful to think,
This vessel can sink,
Icebergs inevitable,
Lifeboats ungettable
Survival not certain,
Nevertheless, I'd hazard a guess.

Yet again we set sail
On the maiden voyage of the Titanic,
This time we assume,
This vessel is doomed,
Icebergs in waves,
No lifeboats to save us,
Survival in doubt,
Nevertheless, I'd hazard a guess.

There will be as many rides
On the maiden voyage of the Titanic,
As you need to convince you,
No ship is unsinkable,
Always another iceberg,
Never enough lifeboats,
You cannot survive;
Nevertheless, the answer I guess.
 The only thing unsinkable
On the maiden voyage of the Titanic -

Was Molly Brown.

Escape from the Great Impasse

This poem is two bits of poetry stitched together. Parts of it are attempts at expanding or improving what eventually became the song s'Argamassa Rain and the rest is snippets of similar sentiment which fitted the pattern. It's just a poem; was never a song, though I think it has possibilities. I don't know where the title came from, although at one stage I appeared to be planning a recording project called "The Great Impasse" which included songs called "Bell of Doom", "Who Cares Anyway?" and "Going in Search of Angels". It looks like it was going to be an intensely religious undertaking, but now it will probably never see the light of day.

Written as s'Argamassa additions during & after May, 1998

Livin' a lazy life of leisure,
Playin' out a crazy game for pleasure,
Makin' the grade measure for measure,
Straying round a maze to claim lost treasure,
No salvation, just damage limitation,
No salvation, just damage limitation.

Flyin' in the frowning face of convention,
Dyin' in the downward race for good intentions,
Denyin' any grounds for chasing perfection,
Cryin' in the howling space left by rejection,
No salvation, just damage limitation,
No salvation, just damage limitation.

Spare me from your preciousness -
You've nothin' new to say,
Cut to the chase, conceal your face;
Just hide your shame away.

The weathervane is set for rain,
The Magic Circle closes,
Protects the few from threats undue,
Where consciousness proposes.

Seal me in my emptiness
of being only me,
No empathy, no ecstasy,
No synchronicity.

No questions asked answers distilled,
The truth is blurred with reason,
No nearer be the dream fulfilled,
Till comes the killing season.

Help me to escape the night
while running from the day;
My work not done, my race not run,
Help me steal away.

You kept the best until the last,
You stored it up and saved it,
And now you've reached the great impasse,
We're all so glad,
We're all so glad,
We're all so glad you made it.
Yes!
We're all so glad you made it.

Alarm

This is a simple lament for the way that the longer you live the faster time seems to just disappear. It appeared as a song on the demo album "Beyond Pure Extremes in November 2000.

Written May 1998

We all have recollections of the days that have gone by;
Easy to perceive inside the winking of an eye.
We all have expectations of the days we have to come;
They're still the outcome of a monumental sum.
But in between then and now
the time has all been swept away somehow.
But in between then and now
the days just seemed to slip away till now.
But in between now and when
the time will go on flying by again.
But in between now and when
the days cascade into a time called then.

We surround ourselves with memories and echoes from the past;
Reminiscence and nostalgia to make the moment last.
In positive belief that our future will be blessed,
We contemplate and celebrate each triumph and success.
But in between then and now
the time has all been swept away somehow.
But in between then and now
the days just seemed to slip away till now.
But in between now and when
the time will go on flying by again.
But in between now and when
the days cascade into a time called then.

Turning Over Stones (Meet the spirit).

A salute to the thorny and sometimes worrying thought that you know when you are not as youthful as you were. I suppose it might be misunderstood as being a "frightened of dying" statement, but if you spend any of your time turning over stones there will sometimes be surprises underneath, both pleasant and disturbing.
Recorded at Amber Studios in September 2000 on the demo album "Only Turning Over Stones".

Written in July, 1998

We're lonely when we turn our heads,
Not hearing where our memories echo from,
And then we wonder at times of solitude,
Where all our good time friends have gone.
One day your heart stops singin';
It seems that time stands still,
Now you can stop and look back upon your life
as if watching from a distant hill.
Then it's time to meet the spirit in the sky,
To be gone,
No chance to turn around and say goodbye to anyone.
Why do we try to find the reason why?
There's not one,
There's not one.

When lowly souls just dream away,
Awake too late just howling at the moon,
And sadness waits for cruel fate;
All because our winter comes too soon.
When loves last brown leaf falls from the tree,
And away inside the wind she sweeps,
New snow will fill this window sill,

And deep upon the hill still sleeps.
Then it's time to meet the spirit in the sky,
To be gone,
No chance to turn around and say goodbye to anyone.
Why do we try to find the reason why?
There's not one,
There's not one

Careworn and windblown; it's only mem'ries we own,
Turning over stones,
We all travel alone; destination unknown,
Turning over stones,
Foolish devil-may-care; rising up to the dare,
Turning over stones,
On a wing and a prayer; searching here, searching there,
Turning over, turning over, only turning over stones.

Down home girl

The idea for this song seemed to have hung around for a long time; possibly since some time in 70's. Eventually it crystallised as a song with a hint of country and western to it, and was recorded at Amber Studios on the demo album "Only Turning Over Stones" in September 2000.

Written July 1998

The hazy grey city sky;
Reflecting sadness in your eyes,
Rushing wind that stings your face,
Telling you you're out of place,
Traffic noise put's your head in a swirl,
You're just a sweet little down home girl.
Yep!
You're just a sweet little down home girl.

Green fields are where you long to be,
Blue skies are what you want to see,
The city just tires you and you long to the free.
Yep!
You're just a sweet little down home girl.
Yep!
You're just a cute little down home girl.

You walk alone across the square,
Your mood and your mind are lost elsewhere,
Beneath your feet the dirty street,
About your ears the city's heat,
And the noise put's your head in a swirl,
You're just a cute little down home girl.
Yep!
You're just a cute little down home girl.

Green fields are where you long to be,
Blue skies are what you want to see,
The city just tires you and you long to the free.
Yep!
You're just a sweet little down home girl.
Yep!
You're just a cute little down home girl.

Once bitten

If you've ever woken up in the middle of the night with an uneasy, frightened feeling, as if there's something sinister afoot, then you may understand this song. From a purely simplistic point of view it's obviously about vampires, and was probably written after watching a film like "The Lost Boys". This was always a song, and was recorded at Amber Studios in September 2000 on the demo album "Only Turning Over Stones".

Written 20th August, 1998

With black flashing daggers reality staggers,
In search of forgotten desires,
Through dark disturbed dreams, where fantasy screams,
In colours that nightmares inspire,
Fast pounds the brave heart; you awake with a start,
As thunderstorm rage in your head,
Cold in this strange room your eyes pierce the gloom,
And you're thankful to still be in bed.
Something strange is happening here,
Something strange, something weird,
Something strange is happening here,
Something strange, something strange.

Is there nothing to fear from the ghosts stranded here?
Lost souls condemned to no peace,
In purgatory taunted, pale, tortured and haunted,
For endless, relentless release.
So trembling in terror you look in the mirror,
Your doorway to hope on the wall,
But filled with new dread, now you've joined the undead;
For you see no reflection at all.
Something strange is happening here,
Something strange, something weird,
Something strange is happening here,
Something strange, something strange.

Garlic smells will repulse you, running water convulse you,
Beware crosses of silver and wood.
Daylight will blind you, and night-time will find you
in unquenchable thirst for fresh blood,
And water once blessed, burns and tears at your flesh,
Leaves you writhing and thrashing in pain,
Wolves howl at the moon, bats fly round the room,
As you wake from your tomb once again.
Something strange is happening here,
Something strange, something weird,
Something strange is happening here,
Something strange, something strange, something strange.

Lightning Source UK Ltd.
Milton Keynes UK
UKOW01f2044080416

271881UK00001B/1/P